AFTERLIFE

There Will Be Trouble

Book 1

PG-Rated Version

E. Vince

ISBN: **979-8-9895430-0-7**

Foreword

In the infinite dimension where dreams amalgamate with eternity, a tale unfolds—one embedded with celestial wisdom and earthly strife. "AFTERLIFE: There Will Be Trouble," penned by the insightful hand of E. Vince, beckons readers into a world beyond the veil, where the ethereal dance of existence continues unabated.

In Vince's narrative, the afterlife is not a serene respite but a vibrant spectrum of experiences, challenges, and revelations. It is a reality where the echoes of earthly tribulations reverberate, and the celestial forces orchestrate a cosmic symphony that transcends the mundane. This is not a realm of idyllic repose but a canvas on which the hues of trouble and triumph converge to paint the portrait of an everlasting journey.

Through this literary pilgrimage, guided by the meticulous prose of E. Vince, we find ourselves entangled with a cast of characters as diverse as the cosmos itself. From the empathetic souls grappling with the intricacies of existence to the celestial beings navigating the delicate balance between duty and compassion, each character breathes new life into this tale.

The subtitle, "There Will Be Trouble," serves as both a harbinger and an invitation. Trouble, in Vince's universe, is not a malevolent force but a catalyst for growth, an incubator in which the essence of the soul is refined. It challenges the characters to confront their deepest fears, question their beliefs, and, ultimately, transcend the limitations of their existence. Philosophy and creativity converge in this literary odyssey, where Vince's narrative prowess guides readers through the labyrinth of metaphysical inquiry. The afterlife becomes a stage, and the characters, both earthly and celestial, are the players in a cosmic drama that explores the fundamental questions of purpose, redemption, and the interconnectedness of all souls.

As you turn the pages of "AFTERLIFE," be prepared to meet both uncertainty and revelation, where the boundaries between the known and the unknown blur. E. Vince, with a masterful stroke of the pen, invites you to ponder the nature of existence itself and to unravel the enigma that is life beyond life.

So, dear reader, brace yourself for an expedition into the uncharted territories of the afterlife—a place where trouble is not to be feared but embraced, for it is within these challenges that the true essence of the soul emerges. E. Vince beckons you to join this celestial sojourn, where trouble is but a prelude to the symphony of eternity.

Apollo Jackson

Preface

This book presents a universal concern of humankind, perhaps the most urgent and important concern of man over all our experience. It is summarily expressed as the well-known trilemma, authorship unknown, but attributed to such ancient philosophers as Epicurus, Tactus, or Carneades: "If God is unable to prevent evil, then He is not omnipotent; if God is not willing to prevent evil, then He is not all-good; if God is both willing and able to prevent evil, then whence cometh evil?"

While a shallow read of the trilemma may seem to garner merit, there are, of course, logical arguments to be made to challenge the premises and implied conclusion (beyond our immediate scope). Whether the syllogism is completely valid or not, this question of the co-existence of a good God and evil has, continues to, and will always occupy human thought. To redress this problem directly, Christianity has developed an apologetic framework, theodicy, the Problem of The Redemption of God. The fundamental tenet of theodicy is human free will. Non-theists and perhaps agnostics will not have an issue with the concept of the redemption of God. However, many theists, especially fundamentalists and more conservative persuasions, may object to the concept. Objections likely will be based on the perceived questioning of God's honor, which is neither intended nor expressed.

The absent, and thus implied, second clause of the subtitle is, *In the Hearts and Minds of a Fallen Humanity*. Ergo, the Redemption of God in the Hearts and Minds of a Fallen Humanity; the implication being that as an imperfect lens distorts a perfect image, we, being imperfect, distort perfection—we cannot help but see error and distortion, even in God, though it is not present.

This brings us to the theme of the book: the redemption of God in our hearts and minds. Perhaps the reader has himself or herself experienced or empathized alongside a friend or loved one who has experienced pain and suffering of such magnitude that they have been forever impacted. And perhaps the reader has questioned God, His goodness, His power, His wisdom, His kindness, etc., in view of this suffering. This book was written as a theodicy to honor God in circumstances of unbearable pain and suffering and as a balm to the hurting, to give hope and bring healing.

The Problem of Heaven. The problem with Heaven is that God abides there, and God certainly eclipses any and all human concerns; thus, it would be difficult, if not impossible, to write a credible narrative about a person or people and their concerns in the presence of God—besides, their concerns would cease to exist in God's presence. So, the concept of Paradise is employed as a prop to give an otherworldly experience while maintaining human concerns and tensions. Paradise, as employed in this book, is not a theological statement but merely freedom of artistic expression.

The Problem of Celebrities. Anyone we meet in Paradise may be subject to readers' opinions and biases towards them, resulting in questioning, "Why was this or that person allowed into Paradise?" Again, freedom of artistic expression and perhaps a bit of optimism are in operation here. Please join in the celebration of some celebrity's virtual salvation that you didn't think made it.

The Problem of Orthodoxy. A plurality of theological aspects of this fictional work will be challenged by many Christians. Please remember, this is fiction, and as Christians, we should be gracious and loving. The quote below is a poignant reminder of the damage to the Lord's reputation and to the Christian witness we do when we behave in an unchristian manner.

> "I received a large number of letters from readers of my books, most of them enthusiastically friendly, some of them helpfully critical, a few nasty or even vicious. And the nastiest of all, I am sorry to report, are almost invariably motivated by religion. Such unchristian abuse is commonly experienced by those who are perceived as enemies of Christianity." Dawkins, *The God Delusion* (New York, NY: Mariner Books, 2006), pp. 241-242.

Here, Richard Dawkins is sharing his experience of enduring an unchristian (nasty and vicious) response from supposed Christians. While it might on the surface seem valiant to defend God, although we may actually only be defending our own narrow views, what in a nasty or vicious person would attract Dawkins to want to investigate the claims of Christianity? How is a nasty or vicious person honoring the Lord?

My point in bringing this up is this work is a work of comfort to the hurting and not a theological text; please do not harm the cause of Christ in someone's journey by reflecting Christianity in your reviews in a nasty or vicious manner. Thank you.

Table of Contents

Part One

Unfinished Business

Chapter 1

Karen gasps for breath every several words. "What kind of God would give me a bad heart?"

"God loves you, Mrs. Hill," Reverend Bilford says. "You've just—"

"My two children," Karen says, sobbing. "What's going to—"

"The real question here is, can I forgive God?" Bert blurts.

"Mr. Hill, I know this is very dif—"

"Difficult? You don't know crap! And you darn sure don't know difficult! You can take your God and his so-called salvation right out of my life and shove it somewhere the sun doesn't shine!" Bert yells as he turns his back on the pastor, paces around the unkept master bedroom, avoiding clothes and medical equipment strewn about, and settles at the window, looking out at a dreary, misting day.

"I can see this is not the time to have this discussion," says the pastor as he heads for the door. "I'll see myself out. So sorry to have disturbed you and added to your pain."

"Ha! Asking God to forgive you!" Bert bellows, directed at Karen. "That's a laugh! It's God who needs to be forgiven for destroying my life!" Bert shouts as he storms out of their bedroom, leaving her crying.

Karen spends several hours praying and thinking, as well as her oxygen-deprived brain could handle. She accepts that there's no hope of a recovery and that she's been a burden for too long to her family.

She makes the final decision of her life with the last and only power she has remaining.

God, if you can hear me, I can't do this anymore. I'm so tired of all the pain. Take me now. Look after Melody, Roy, and Bert for me. Please forgive me for failing as a mother and wife, Karen cries silently to God.

***

The next day, Bert wakes Karen at the usual time. "Here. Take these."

"What? Oh, no. No more pills," says Karen.

"I don't have time for this, Karen. My head's killing me—"

"No, no."

"Please, for the kids. They need y—"

"No, no good anymore. Can't mother (more sobs). Can't wife. No good. Want be done." Karen struggles to get the words out.

"I don't know what to do anymore," Bert says. After a brief pause, he adds, "And I'm so tired of always having to be everything, father, mother, husband, wife, everything. You need to do your part, Karen! Take your darn pills and help me!"

Karen shakes her head. "No, sorry, so sorry."

Bert slams the front door as he leaves the house, late to work (again), blaming Karen (again), and conveniently forgetting that he overslept due to a hangover (again).

***

The next day, Saturday morning, Bert helps Karen get cleaned up a bit and somewhat dressed. "Okay, Karen, can't you sit up just a little higher? It hurts my back to keep bending over. Sit up," Bert insists. Karen's sitting propped up in bed and even combs her hair part-way through. Bert's just fed the kids a cold breakfast and returned to Karen's room with Roy (their youngest).

"Okay, that's good enough," Bert tells Karen as his impatience grows, watching her try to put a comb through a small section of her dirty hair.

"Good morning, Mom," says Roy. "You're dressed and sitting up. It's nice to see you dressed. Momma, I can't find my snowsuit."

"Sorry, I can't get, Roy."

"Mom, why are you always sick?"

"Sorry," Karen says, sobbing. "You don't deserve this," she gasps. "I do anything makeup you and Melody."

"It's okay, Mom. I didn't mean to make you cry. I just want God to make you well. I pray for God to make you better every day. Why doesn't He make you better?"

"Oh my gosh, what is it, Karen? Are you all right?" Bert asks. "Roy, go out to the car and wait for me. Now!" Turning toward her, he anxiously says, "Karen?" This is in response to an expression of significant pain and deeper discoloration on Karen's face. Bert adjusts the oxygen up, and Karen responds a bit after about a minute. Bert notices that Karen's oxygen tube is kinked. "You're gonna hafta be more careful with your darn tube; I can't be in here every minute of the day and night," Bert fusses.

Karen cries for a moment and then addresses Bert. "Haven't mothered kids years. Dying, never chance make up. Just children. Need much. So unfair."

"Look, a heart could still become avai—"

"No, won't. Stop, Bert. Got face it. Dying. Meds not work. No heart. Too weak transpl—. Got face it. Prepare kids."

Bert grinds his teeth as Karen speaks the truth, pausing twice every sentence to catch her breath. Roy comes back in from the car parked in the garage.

"Dad? Are we goin—"

"Yes, Roy. Just give me a darn minute." Roy's father tries to regain some composure.

"Go," says Karen. "Take Roy Snow Hill. Promised." Bert nods his head and walks out of their bedroom.

Thinking silently as well as she possibly can considering her condition, Karen says to God, *Why did You give me children only to take them away? I only want to be a good mother to my kids. I can't leave my son hanging like this! You are making me abandon my daughter right when she needs me the most. How can You do this to my family? How can You do this to me? What have I done to deserve this? How can You claim to be the All-Loving God?*

Chapter 2

The following Thursday, as Karen and Bert enter the cardiology clinic, Bert hits a pothole in the parking lot with the wheelchair, the oxygen tank falls, and the tubing detaches, breaking the connector and interrupting Karen's oxygen flow. "What the heck happened? I had that darn bottle strapped tight," Bert complains. Bert tries but cannot fix the tube in the broken connector, so he curses and flails about in frustration. A nurse observes the commotion just outside the entrance and calls another nurse, and they both rush out to assist. One of them flies back in to get another connector, and soon the commotion subsides.

"There, Mr. Hill, it's all better now. Take a couple of deep breaths," one of the nurses says to Bert. The other focuses on Karen. The nurses escort Karen and Bert into the lobby, and once out of hearing range, the younger nurse says to the older, "What's his problem?"

They're called back immediately to Karen's cardiologist's perfectly sterile, windowless office with scores of books neatly arranged by size and color, and a hospital chaplain is there. The chaplain stands as the Hills enter. After brief introductions, the cardiologist begins, "Karen, your heart condition has been class IV-D, the final stage of your congenital heart disease, for just over six months. There is nothing more that medicine can do for you; there's no chance for a heart, but even if we found one, you're not a transplant candidate. I'm so sorry, Mrs. and Mr. Hill. It's my recommendation that you act quickly to get your affairs in order. The rate of progression of the disease is increasing. I do not advise any delay. I also recommend consideration of a hospice. There is excellent hospice care at the Palliative Plato Care Center. And in-home hospice care is—"

"How am I supposed to take care of two kids by myself? And work, and clean the house, and make ends meet?" Bert rants.

"Bert. Bert," Karen says softly, motioning her hand slowly to try to get Bert's attention. Failing this, she just weeps.

As Bert seems oblivious to Karen's distress and the doctor's and chaplain's pleas for calm, the chaplain finally takes Bert by the arm. "Mr. Hill, please! Can't you see your wife's distress at all this anger?"

Bert cries out, "I'm dying here too! It's not just Karen, ya know. I'm gonna lose everything!" Bert just gets up and leaves the office. Storming into the lobby, he lights up a cigarette and heads into the parking lot, kicking over a small wastebasket in the process.

Karen just quietly sobs, too out of breath and exhausted to engage. The chaplain gently speaks up again. "I'm so sorry. This isn't fair. This isn't right. You and your husband need some time to grieve and mourn together. When you're able to speak, please give me a call." The chaplain hands Karen his card and a card for the local in-home hospice care provider. "In-home hospice is good for some families, but I'm not sure if it's a good fit for you. I'm not comfortable Bert will be able to give you the care you'll need," the chaplain says.

The doctor calls in the nurse and hands her a script to give to Bert for Xanax and one for Ambien to help him through this distressing time. Another nurse helps Karen to the car, and they leave the clinic, Karen sobbing and Bert fuming.

Still on the way home, Karen stops crying and says, "Need to say goodbye."

"What? What are you talking about?" asks Bert.

"Already feel being off meds. Not much time." Even this tiny amount of discourse is tiring, as Karen gasps for breath after every few words. "You remarry, deserve life. Kids need mom touch. You no clue how raise teenage girl. You outgunned." Karen smiles for the first time in days. "You need help, remarry."

"That's just ridiculous; I can't remarry. There's no point in talking about it."

Karen's turning a bit more bluish and is slower and more chopped in her speech. "Build relation kids. Loving, gentle. No much discipl—." Stopping for over a minute after turning up her oxygen to the maximum flow and catching her breath, Karen continues, "Talk open, no lecture, listen kids. No hard them, let be kids. Fun, enjoy each other, be family (pointing to self) proud of." Karen's voice is down to a whisper. She collapses in her seat but remains conscious.

"Yeah, yeah," Bert says tritely. Bert pulls into the driveway, but Karen's too exhausted to get out of the car for a while, so they just sit 'til she recovers a bit. Karen feels Bert fuming at the growing burden and inconvenience of her plight. Karen thinks to herself, *Bert's a good man who's suffered because of me. If I was the wife and mother I should have been, he would have been a happy husband and father. It hurts to see him so miserable. God, please give my family the peace and joy they never experienced because of me.*

"Bert," Karen whispers as she's wheeled from the garage back into the house, pointing to Bert and slowly shaking her head *no*, "make dinner by yourself. Ask Melody."

"Melody's in her room with the door shut and on the phone, like she always is. I'll just do it myself. Do you want something?"

Bert wheels Karen to the living room and walks down the hall to Melody's room. "Melody"—knocking on the door—"come out here for a moment," Bert says.

"Yes, Daddy?" Sounding somewhat frustrated, she asks, "What is it now?"

"Dinner will be ready in about twenty minutes. Set the table and get your brother into the bathroom. Then go see your mother."

"I can't believe it! Homecoming's just an hour away, and I have to get ready. I don't have time to eat, and I certainly don't have time to babysit my preteen brother! Why can't I have a life?"

"I told you to get out here, set the table, and get your brother ready. You will have dinner, and you will cut the crap! Now!"

"I hate this family!" She speaks under her breath as she storms down the hall to Roy's bedroom. *This is Mom's job!* Melody says to herself. Why do I have to suffer just because I have a mother who's too sick to do anything? (Bang, bang, bang!) "Roy! Get in the bathroom and wash your hands! Dinner's almost ready."

"I don't want dinner; leave me alone," Roy cries.

"You crying again? You dork! Why do I have to live in this family? (bang, bang, bang) You better do it, dork, or I'm telling your father." Melody then heads to her mother, who's sitting in her wheelchair in the living room, oxygen and tears flowing.

Karen motions to Melody to come closer. Karen adapts to her condition by supplementing her spoken words with makeshift signs. "How (pointing to Melody), honey? I love you," Karen signs.

"Yeah, Mom, I love you too. I'm so sorry you have to go through all this. Look, we'll talk later. I have to get ready for homecoming. I missed the last homecoming, remember? See you later, Mom." Melody makes no eye contact.

On his way to the living room, Bert collides with Melody as she heads back to her room. No words, no eye contact. Bert walks into the living room toward the credenza upon which the decanters sit.

Karen whispers to Bert as he pours himself a tall double before dinner and then puts the frozen pizza in the oven. "Going be hard.

Need tell kids. Help understand." Bert ignores Karen's uncomfortably twisted body in her wheelchair. "Not much time. Use time help kids accept." Bert nods and heads over to the decanter to pour himself another. While waiting for the pizza, he has yet another. When the pizza's ready, he calls the children, helps Karen to the kitchen table, and turns her oxygen back up to maximum flow (just in case).

"Melody, you forgot napkins. Get 'em," Bert says as the kids arrive at the table. Roy turns his head toward Melody and sticks his tongue out at her.

"Okay, listen up. Your mother has something to tell you over dinner. Listen before you start asking questions. And listen carefully; you know your mother's voice is down to a whisper." Bert slurs in his drunken state.

"Good news, I bet. I'm really adopted, and my real parents—" snipes Melody.

"Shut up! Didn't you hear a thing I said? This is serious—" Bert says.

"Please! Please!" Karen whispers. She takes a minute to try to recover her breath. "I'm dying. (slowly shakes head 'no') Can do about. All (signing 'I') want before die (pointing to each family member) be okay. Love. Patient. Good."

Yeah, sure. Anything else I should put on my plate? Bert thinks to himself as he belches 80-proof. The kids nod their heads 'yes' in response to their mother. Then Bert turns to the children.

"Your mother's heart disease is worser every day. We don't know how long she has, but she made the decision to hospie, hospee," Bert mumbles.

"Hospice," Karen whispers.

"What's that?" Roy asks through tears.

"It means that your mother is going off her medications and only taking pain pills, and she'll do it at home and die right in front of us. Isn't that the way good families are supposed to do it?" Bert slurs.

"Then Mommy won't be in so much pain?" asks Roy through tears, ignoring his father's absurdity, and looking at Melody.

"No, she won't be in any pain. I'll be in plenty of it, but she won't. She's check'n out on us," Bert continues in sarcasm.

"Then she'll get better?" asks Roy.

"No, you dork! Don't you get it?" Melody says. "Our mother isn't going to get any better. The pain pills will take away her pain, but she's still going to die—"

"Roy, Melody, (signing 'self') dying. Short time left. Import—. Now say goodbye. Be good each other."

"No, Mommy, no. I don't want you to die. God won't let you die. I prayed for God to make you better," Roy cries, gets up, and hugs his mother gently.

"You're ten or eleven years old; that's old enough to face the facts. Stop whining!" Bert commands. "Oh darn, the pizza's getting cold."

"Stop! Let kids feel. Let feelings—" Karen turns again to the kids. "(signing 'I') feel same. I (slowly shaking head 'no') leave you. I stay, be your mom. That's (slowly shaking head 'no') happen. Goodbye, my sweet loves."

"I'm so sorry, Mom," cries Melody as she runs into her room, collects her things, and bolts out the door to head for the homecoming game, her mascara smearing down her face just a bit. After dinner, Karen suggests that Bert invite his parents to stay with them for a while to help. He does so, and they arrive the next afternoon.

Chapter 3

Karen's in her wheelchair in the living room, watching one of her favorite shows, when the doorbell rings. Bert answers. "I wish we could have come sooner, son, but we didn't know when anyone would be home to let us in," Grandma Hill says as they enter the Hill home.

"I'm so glad you could make it," Bert says, welcoming his parents. "You'll take the guest room in the basement. I'll bring your luggage down."

"We're so sorry, son, for all this. It's a terrible thing for you and the kids," Grandpa Hill says.

"It's bad for Karen too," Grandma says quietly to Grandpa.

"It's not as bad for her as it is for me, that's for darn sure," Bert says, not seeming to care whether Karen hears or not.

Bert's combination of alcohol smell and callousness is apparent to his parents. "Son, have you been drinking? It's a little early for that, isn't it?" his mother asks. Bert doesn't respond or acknowledge her.

Chapter 4

A couple of days later, Karen has a rare burst of energy in one of her more lucid moments. She takes advantage of it and wants to speak to the kids, so she turns up the oxygen. She needs to say goodbye just one more time while she's able. Roy's back from school and doing his math homework. Karen knows Roy will soon come in to see her; he checks on her about every forty minutes during waking hours when he's home.

Roy knocks and enters his mom's bedroom. Karen uses a combination of whispers and made-up sign language to try to communicate with Roy. "Sorry (signing 'I') won't be around, be your mother. Want be (pointing at Roy) mother more anything world. (Signing 'I'), too sick. Not (pointing at Roy) fault (shaking head slowly 'no'). (Signing 'I'), miss you so much, son."

Roy just cries, hugs his mother, and says, "I love you, Mom. I'm going to miss you more than anything."

Karen continues, "Take care Daddy, Sister. No forget care (pointing at Roy)."

"I will, Mommy."

Roy kisses his mom, and she asks him to ask his sister to come see her. After a few minutes, Melody walks into the bedroom. "Yes, Mother? Do you need something? I hope you don't have to go to the bathroom again."

"Melody (Karen motions to come closer). Sorry, (signing 'I') wasn't mother (pointing at Melody) needed. (Signing 'I'), never healthy model, mistakes with (pointing at Melody). Please forgive (signing 'me').”

“Whatever. It’s all good. Is that it?”

“(Signing 'self'), love you, want (pointing at Melody) good life. You valuable (signing 'self'). Derek mistake—”

“I can’t believe it! You called me in here for that! Derek and I love each other, and you’re just jealous. You can’t stand it that I have a man that loves me. I’m not going to stand here and listen to this. And don’t you ever talk about Derek that way again, or you’re not my mother!”

Melody storms out of her mom’s bedroom, leaving her mother in tears and broken in spirit, crushed at the thought that this might be their last opportunity to say goodbye and have it end like this.

Still crying, Karen hears the doorbell ring and Grandma Hill letting someone in the door.

“I’m Chaplain Spears from the clinic. You must be Ada; we spoke briefly earlier today.”

“Yes, please come in. My daughter-in-law is in her bedroom. I’ll help her into the wheelchair and bring her out. Would you like some tea while you wait?”

Grandma makes some tea and escorts the chaplain to the living room. After a few minutes, Grandma brings Karen into the room juxtaposed with the chaplain for conversation. Grandma Hill then brings Karen some tea, freshens the chaplain’s tea, and leaves them alone. They’ll have about an hour or so before Bert’s due home from work.

“Thank you for coming,” Karen says in a gentle whisper. Chaplain Spears adjusts his cane-back chair right up to her.

“No problem, Mrs. Hill. I’m glad your mother-in-law called me. Is there anything specific you wanted to talk about?” Karen nods her head 'yes.'

"(Signing 'I') want confess and pray family."

"You know that I'm not Catholic, Mrs. Hill. I didn't think you came from a Catholic background—which doesn't matter to me—but I can't hear your confession formally if you're thinking of it in a Catholic sense."

Karen shakes her head slowly. "No, Catholic. Want get right God before die."

"I see. Well then, that I can help you do. What do you want to repent for before God, Mrs. Hill?"

"(Signing 'I' and beginning to cry) failed mother, wife. So sorry!"

"You haven't failed, Mrs. Hill. From what I can see, you've been a wonderful wife and mother to your family. God is not upset with you."

"Melody hates (signing 'me'). Bert resents (signing 'me'). Roy, still little boy, needs mother (signing 'I') abandon him."

"You're all in so much pain (*Lord, give me wisdom and strength,* the chaplain silently prays). The Lord loves you, Karen, and He will take care of your family. I promise you that. It won't be easy for them, but the Lord won't let them go."

Karen's weeping profusely. Chaplain Spears puts his arms around her and begins to pray: "Dear Heavenly Father, lift this dear sister's heavy burdens. Make Your presence and love for her and each of her family members apparent. Reassure her of Your love. Speak peace into her heart and home, dear Lord. And please give her strength to continue to be the good mother and wife this family needs. Let her know she's done a good job and You're well pleased with her, Lord. And I ask a special request for Karen, Lord; please give her a compassionate guardian angel, someone to watch over her and escort her safely into Your arms. We ask this in Jesus' name. Amen."

Karen nods 'yes' and 'thank you' through tears. "(Signing 'I,' still crying from the prayer) decide home hospice. Hospice nurse, come today." The conversation goes on for a few minutes. Karen feels some peace.

Chaplain Spears sees himself out after their prayer time just as the hospice staff and men from the medical equipment company arrive with a special bed, a new and larger continuous oxygen generator, and other equipment. The men set up the bed and equipment in the rec room. The nurse helps Karen into the new bed and makes her as comfortable as possible. Karen and the nurse discuss a few things, and then the nurse asks if she's ready for her first dose of oral morphine. Karen responds, "Yes."

***

Later that day, Karen's at home in her hospice bed in the rec room. Bert has not come home yet. The hospice nurse is on the phone giving her report to the charge nurse. "She's had her first dose and sleeping well; it's a blessing. Urinary output is almost zero; color is a pale brown and cloudy; she's swollen in her extremities, and she can't get warm. She's having some confusion. Patient's mother-in-law is here…"

Chapter 5

Later that day, in the early evening, Bert returns from work, and he socializes briefly with his parents before he continues drinking. Bert's been enjoying happy hour every day after work. "Mom, Dad, thanks for coming. I really needed your help. Karen can't do anything; I've been late for work almost every day since I can't remember when, and the kids missed the bus a couple times already last week. It's just crazy," Bert says to his parents.

"We understand, son. We'll take care of the house and kids so you can focus on Karen's comfort. Now I've got some cleaning and organizing to finish in the kids' rooms. It's been so busy around here today. What, with the chaplain's visit and the hospice people coming and going, I haven't had a moment to get anything done," Grandma says as she and Bert walk into Roy's room.

"My, this is a disaster, son. Perhaps we'll be able to see Roy's floor sometime soon? He has no clean socks or underwear and no long pants, either," Grandma says as she rummages through Roy's belongings. "Ah! Here they are. No, these are filthy. I'll start with the laundry."

"Thanks, Mom. I'm sure it's no better in Melody's room. I just haven't had time to—"

"Of course not, son. Don't worry about it; I'll take care of it. Now, go tell Melody to set her laundry by the washer. I'll get it going and then start dinner."

"Well, son," Grandpa says, coming in from surveying the outside of the house. "I saw some cracked siding, and a few weeds need pull'n, but it's too cold out there, so I'll change the burned-out bulbs and get to work on the siding tomorrow. That siding isn't going anywhere soon."

"Okay, thanks, Dad. Whatever you want to do is fine with me."

Chapter 6

Grandma reaches out to the Hill family's church for support. Bert and his parents are in his pastor's office discussing issues surrounding Karen's soon passing. "I want to apologize again, Mr. Hill, for upsetting you last week—" Pastor Bilford says.

Ignoring the pastor's remarks, Bert says, "I don't know what to do anymore. All this fuss over Karen. It's great for her, but I'm hurting too, and nobody's lifting a finger to help me!" He is sitting between his parents, but they just stay silent.

"Bert, of course you don't know what else to do, and you're in tremendous pain right now. And so are the kids and Karen. You've never been through this before. It's the hardest thing anyone ever does. It's never easy," says the pastor. "I've been across this desk from what seems like scores of families facing this same issue. Yet each time, my heart breaks anew with the struggle of loved ones. The good news is that Karen knows the Lord, and the Lord is faithful to His promises. Karen will soon be with Him, and all her pain and limitations will be a thing of the past, forever."

"Right, her troubles will soon be over, but mine are getting worse!" Bert snaps.

"Bert!" Bert's mother responds. "We didn't raise you like that." Bert's father ignores Bert's outburst, acknowledges the pastor's words, thanks him, and then asks, "We've never been through this either. What is going to happen, pastor? Will Karen be in any pain?"

"No, I don't believe she will. Bert, Karen's getting pain medication, right?" asks the pastor. Bert nods his head. "The meds will keep Karen comfortable; in fact, she may lose consciousness and never wake up. It'll be like going to sleep; she'll be sleeping and then just stop breathing. Then shortly after that, her heart will stop, and her complexion will change; it'll be apparent that her spirit has left her body, and she'll be with our Lord."

"How can we best help?" asks Bert's mother.

"Bert's going to be grieving for quite some time to come. It will be hard for Bert to function and keep the house running. If you can help him keep the house running smoothly, that'll be a great help, Mrs. Hill. By the way, I understand from the Ladies Auxiliary that they plan to bring meals to the house three days each week for a while. They usually bring the dinner by 5 p.m., and there's usually enough for supper that night and lunch for the next day."

"That will be very helpful. Please thank the ladies for us," Grandma says.

"Of course, Mrs. Hill. And (looking back toward Bert), how are the kids handling the situation?" asks the pastor.

Bert, gaining a modicum of composure in response to his mother's admonition, says, "Fine, just fine, I believe."

"And look, I want to apologize again for upsetting you and Mrs. Hill. I just wanted to look into Karen's spiritual comfort. I had no intention of causing you any more pain than you're already in; I want you to know that," says Pastor Bilford.

Chapter 7

The next morning, Bert's up and getting ready for work. "Oh darn! I can't believe I did that." After a moment's pause, Bert mumbles under his breath, "I wish I could get rid of this darn headache!"

"What, son?" asks Grandma as she sets a bowl of cereal on the table for Bert.

"Nothing. Oh, I just put salt in my coffee. Heck, I don't care. I'm gonna drink it." A few spits and sputters later, he continues, "I guess I'm not. I probably don't need any coffee anyway. I'm late for work."

Bye! Thanks for getting the kids off to school, taking care of the dishes, and letting your own garden go to ruin while you're away, Grandma says sarcastically to herself. *I don't know what's happening to my boy. He was never so selfish or insensitive. He's becoming a stranger.*

***

Later that day, when Bert arrives from work, Roy's in his room, and Melody hasn't come home yet from school.

"Hello, son," Grandpa says to Bert. "How was work? Oh, that fellow from the bank called again today."

"Oh, crap! Can't they just leave me alone for one minute!" Bert shuffles through the mail quickly before he goes over to the credenza. "Bills, bills, bills, bills, crap! This is killing me!"

"Son, your mother and I can help out a—"

"Thanks, Dad, but no. This is my prob—"

"Nonsense, son. This is a family problem. How much do you need to help keep things going?"

"I don't know Dad. I don't know; maybe five thousand or seven thousand will get me through this. But I hate to borrow money from you and Mom."

"This is not a loan, son; this is our part in helping our family. It's the least we can do. I'll write you a check, and you deposit it tomorrow and take some pressure off. You better go see Karen. She's mostly been asleep all day; stirred a couple times. Her color looks a little worse to me."

"Thanks, Dad, it will take a lot of pressure off," Bert responds. Bert starts thinking, *I'll make one back payment and the current payment on the house, the same on the car, a thousand on Karen's medical bills. That'll leave a couple thousand for me. I need to take care of myself.*

***

Bert comes home this Thursday, appearing very tired from work. Things had not gone too well, and after an informal greeting to his mother, Bert sits down in his recliner. "Good evening, son. How was your day? Better, I hope. Aren't you going to look in on Karen?"

Bert ignores his mother. The phone rings. "Yes, this is Bert Hill; who's calling?"

"This is Mr. Brad Foriet from Everyone's Bank. Mr. Hill, you missed last month's payment, and now this month's payment—"

"What the heck are you idiots doing? I sent the bank a letter and told them my wife's dying of heart failure, and I need a little time—"

"We have the letter, Mr. Hill, but the bank—"

"Listen, you Royal Canadian arse, I'm sending in both payments tomorrow, so get off my back! Don't ever call me again. And if you or any of your friends from the bank come snooping around my house,

I'll introduce you to my friends Smith & Wesson. Got it?" He slams the phone on the cradle. "I need a drink!" Bert exclaims.

"Oh, son, that wasn't right," Bert's father admonishes.

"The heck it wasn't! Those leeches have made thousands of dollars off me, and now that I need a little help from them, they turn me down for a loan to help make ends meet and then step up the collection calls! I hate those arses! I hope there's a purgatory!"

"You don't mean that, son. Now look, I think you woke up Karen," says Grandpa.

Oh God, that's all I need, he says to himself as he heads for the rec room. *Now I'll have to clean her up again.*

"Go back to sleep," Bert says as Karen motions.

"What's wrong?" Karen asks.

"Nothing, just go back to sleep. Here, take this," Bert says as he gives her another dropper of oral morphine. *It's easier than cleaning you up,* Bert mumbles to himself.

Bert sits in the chair, and as Karen falls back to sleep, he prays angrily, "I've been good all my life. Why are you punishing me? What have I ever done to You? I tried to give my family a good life, and it's all turning out like crap! What did I do to deserve this? Why don't you help me now when I really need it?"

Back in the living room, Grandma says to Grandpa, "You seem pretty upset after Bert's fight with the bank. All this raw emotion seems to have routed your constitution sugar-plumb. Let's go into the kitchen."

"Yeah, I can't be of any more use here. I'll head back home in the morning."

"You've helped a lot, old man, and I appreciate your being here. But I'll get you packed up tonight, and you can leave tomorrow after Bert goes to work. The only thing left is Karen's passing, and I don't think you'll take that very well."

"I always liked that girl. She was a real treasure. Bert should have treated her better."

"I agree with you. But it's universally true of all husbands, especially you, old man! Go visit Roy and Melody when she gets home."

Grandma silently acknowledges Grandpa's emotional discomfort with that *Oh well, at least that's one less mouth-to-feed* look on her face. *No peaceful passing for Karen or anyone else in her home*, Grandma Hill says to herself. Grandma catches a glimpse of Melody making a beeline for her room out of her peripheral vision. *That girl's in some kind of trouble*, Grandma thinks to herself. She heads over to Melody's room and listens outside the door.

"Yeah, can you believe it? She had the gall to wear his sweater in front of April! I think she's a tramp. Yeah, I cut third and fourth periods today. Hillary had some pot, and we smoked it in the third-floor john. It was great. But have you heard Derek is pressing me to go all the way! (dueling squeals) I want to so bad; we're so in love, but I'm just not sure. Whatever, girl! And, like I said, I wouldn't be caught dead in that dress. I'm wearing my new dress to the prom …

"Wait a minute, someone's knocking at my door. I can't get a minute's peace around here. I need a life; I hate this family—" Melody continues until she can no longer ignore the knocking.

"Yes, Grandma? Can't you see I'm busy now?"

"Melody, don't speak to me like that, child. Have some respect for your elders."

"Yeah, right, whatever!" Melody answers.

"I want to talk to you about your mother," Grandma says.

"Hey, girl, this is gonna take a while. I'll call you back," Melody tells the friend on the phone.

Melody gestures to her grandma, inviting her to enter her room. "Melody, your mother's dying, and you don't seem to care," Grandma says. (Melody's eyes rolling back in her head, head bobbing from front to back, and a pained groan.) "You don't spend any time with your mother. Why not?"

"I do spend time with her. Of course, I care. I just can't be crying my eyes out 24/7, okay? I have a life, too. And my mother has ruined it. I missed the last homecoming because Mom was sick again! Everyone at school thinks I'm such a dork because of my dork family! Why does this have to be my family?"

"Melody, you're so unbelievably selfish. I can scarcely believe the words coming out of your mouth. Your mother loves you, and she loved you all your life. She'd give her right arm for you, child. Why are you disrespecting her and your family so much? The very people who love you, you're shutting them out of your life, especially God—"

"God is the only one that's ruined my life more than my mom. I hate God! I hate this family! It's been really nice talking to you, Grandma. Now, get out of my room and get out of my life!"

Melody rudely escorts her grandma to the door, slams it shut, and then dials her friend. "Yeah, girl, you won't believe what just happened…"

Chapter 8

Later that evening, Grandma has Melody and Roy do the dishes after dinner. "Why are you always mad?" Roy asks Melody as he hands her a rinsed plate.

"Mind your own business, you alien-jerk!" Melody snaps.

"I just asked a question. Mom's sick, and all you care about are your friends and D-e-r-r-e-k-k-k," Roy replies.

"And why shouldn't I? My friends care about me, and Derek loves me. In this family, it's always about Dad, and Mom, and you!"

"That's not true!"

"It is true! And I know why—it's because Mom had you! That's why her heart is garbage! When you were born, it took all her heart strength, and she's been sick ever since! Mom and I had a good relationship before you were born! We did everything together. I wish you were never born!"

Roy takes off like a bat outta you-know-where for his room and weeps bitterly, consumed in grief for being born and causing his mother to lose all her heart strength. Like Melody, Roy spends a good deal of time in his room. Unlike Melody, Roy spends much of that time crying and praying to God, sometimes in great yet sincere anger. "Dear God. Why don't you make my mother well? Why does she have to have a sick heart? Please make her healthy. You can give her my heart. If you don't help her, I won't love You or pray to You anymore. Mrs. Philips, my Sunday school teacher, always says, 'You're good.' If You are good, then please be good to my mom."

***

The next day, Bert comes home from another difficult day at work and starts to drink as soon as he gets in the door, as though he were being driven by something beyond himself to do so. He's nearly drunk before dinner again, which is a daily occurrence.

"Come on, Bert, dinner's get'n cold," Grandma says.

"I'm not hungry tonight," Bert fires back.

"You need to eat something, son."

"I said I'm not hungry. Leave me alone."

"Well, at least come say grace for the kids and me."

"I ain't praying to a God that does this to me! He can go to heck for all I care!"

"Don't listen, children. Your father's so upset, he doesn't mean a word he's saying. He'll be fine in the morning."

"I do mean it!" Bert shouts as he grabs the bottle and heads for his bedroom, slamming the door as he exits the family space.

Chapter 9

The hospice nurse comes up from the rec room where she was tending Karen, pretending that she didn't hear the foul ranting. "I'm sorry to disturb your dinner, but Karen's resting peaceably now, so I'll leave for the night and be back in the early afternoon."

"Would you like some dinner, dear? There's plenty," Grandma offers.

"No thanks. It smells good, though," the nurse responds.

"Is my mommy going to die tonight?" asks Roy.

"You're such a jerk!" Melody snaps.

"Children!" Grandmother intervenes. "Don't argue in front of our guest."

"I don't know, Roy. It won't be long. But your mother won't be in any pain; when she dies, it'll just be like going to sleep. Pray for her," the nurse responds and politely leaves.

Part Two

Ten Again

Chapter 10

It's a balmy minus 15 degrees Fahrenheit, and the sun is painfully bright. There's an inestimably great expanse of pure white to the north, east, and south. A few miles to the west is an immeasurable dark blue expanse punctuated by white forms. Here, on a lonely vigil, two diligent souls are working.

"I don't understand why His Lordship loves man. Even the best of man is corrupt when they shine; and the blackness of their hearts, who can fathom?" asks Jaynes as he briefly lifts his head, turning toward Sarai while continuing to count Emperor penguins that make it into the water just off the West Ice Shelf of Antarctica.

"It is a mystery, but The Majesty does love man. So, there must be some reason, some value they possess that we just don't perceive," responds Sarai.

"Surely, but I just can't grasp why His Lordship ascribes value to man. Man's ruining the Earth, decimating all forms of life, and misappropriating the Earth's resources, acting as if he created them. Of course, the evil man commits toward man is worse by far; there's no bastion of man's heart that evil does not foul. It just seems that His Lordship would do better to give His love and grace to these penguins. At least they would have the decency to show some gratitude!" After a brief pause, Jaynes says, "Interesting. I just received direction to report back. It seems like I have been assigned to a new job."

"Keep in touch, friend," responds Sarai.

E. Vince

"I will. Will you be alright here alone without me?" Jaynes asks. Sarai just gives Jaynes a look. "I'll catch up with you," Jaynes says as he musters to headquarters.

Chapter 11

At Karen's home, they rarely turn on the lights in the rec room, and the curtains remain shut. The hospice nurse feels that Karen rests better with little ambient light. Karen's visitors are mostly Roy, Grandma, and the hospice nurse, who changes a couple of times a day, one early in the day and the other later.

Karen's been on morphine for several days now, and I've had to increase the dosage twice already. She better say her last goodbyes soon, Nurse Molly thinks to herself as she adjusts Karen's pillows. "Are you all right, Mrs. Hill?" asks the nurse, responding to a deep scowl contorting Karen's face.

"What?" whispers Karen.

"How much pain are you in on a scale of one to ten?"

"Dizzy, head sick, heart hurts, can't breathe—"

"I know. I've adjusted the morphine." A few minutes later, the nurse asks, "There, you should start feeling better soon. Would you like some water?"

Karen nods her head in gratitude. "Thank you. What's (pointing at nurse) name? I forget. Sorrrr—" Karen falls asleep quickly due to the morphine. The hospice nurse lets herself out.

When Karen lightens up an hour or so later, she's in a good deal of discomfort and feels the morphine must be increased again, but before it is, she wants to see each family member one last time. So, she asks Roy, who was by her bedside reading her a story when she awoke, to "Get Daddy, Melody. Tell come a few minutes." So, Roy dutifully runs out of his mommy's makeshift bedroom, searching for his father and sister.

"Melody, Mommy wants you. Now, in her room. Hurry up, she's asking for you and Dad."

"My real name is Crescenda; I told you that last night. Can't you see I'm on the phone," Melody yells. "I'm sorry, Starshine, it's just my little twerp brother ruining my life as usual—"

"Melody! I mean Crescenda! Mommy is asking for you. Now."

"Oh, crap! I gotta go, or I'll never have any peace. I'll call you right back."

"Go see what Mom wants. I'll go find Dad," Roy says.

Bert is in his easy chair watching something when Roy bursts in. "Dad, Dad!"

"What the Sam Hill is it? Can't I get one moment's peace around here? Whittaya want now?"

"Momma's asking for you, Dad. She wants you now, please."

"Ah, heck. I just cleaned her up this morning; it's not time for that again. Can't ever get any peace around here." Bert continues to gripe as they move toward the bedroom. "I was just watching the news; darn Republicans. Well, what is it now?"

"Bert, want to see. Not much longer. Need more (morphine). Pain bad. (Pointing to self.) Say goodbye before increase," whispers Karen.

Bert waves his arm to motion the kids over to Karen (Bert stands behind the kids). "Don't strain yourself trying to speak too much. Your color's not very good," Bert says tersely.

"Kids, so sorry. Love (pointing to kids) so much. (Signing 'I'), no do things mother supposed to. (Pointing to kids) Do for each other, (a moment to breathe) love, kind to (pointing to each one in turn). Goodbye, my loves." Karen's now bluish from straining to speak and unable to say anything to Bert.

Roy openly weeps and hugs his frail mother. Melody stands back but waves goodbye and wipes a tear off her cheek from her right eye. Bert dispassionately gives her an increased dosage of oral morphine and thinks to himself: *Oh God; I hope I've cleaned her up for the last time.*

***

The next day, Karen isn't conscious, but Bert continues to give morphine to ensure she doesn't develop pain—he claims. The hospice nurse stops by, takes vitals, and indicates "Perhaps just a few more hours or a day."

Karen's parents arrive later that afternoon. Grandma McCarthy makes supper for the family and straightens the kids' rooms a bit, and Grandpa McCarthy takes Roy for a walk (Melody would have no part of it). "I'm sorry," Grandpa says to Roy, "we would have arrived sooner, but Grandma had bad flu, and we didn't want to make things worse."

"I understand," Roy responds to Grandpa McCarthy. "I'm just glad you're here now."

"I want you to know your mom will be going to heaven soon and be with Jesus. Do you understand, Roy? She won't be in any more pain."

"I'm glad for that. Mom's been sick a long time," Roy says, "but why didn't God make mommy better? I prayed a hundred times."

"I don't know, Roy. Your grandma and I prayed, too, as well as many other people. But God alone chooses to heal or not. God chooses when each person dies. We don't understand, but we must trust God. It's hurtful, but God knows best."

"Maybe God was mad at me because Mommy got sick when I was born," confesses Roy.

"No, son, your momma's heart condition was always a health issue, even many years before she got married. You had nothing to do with your momma getting sick. Do not blame yourself," Grandpa responds.

Grandpa and Roy continue their long, slow walk in the familiar neighborhood past houses and street corners Roy had passed without a care in the world when he was younger. This time, his cares are for his mother and too burdensome to bear, but with Grandpa's help, Roy feels a little peace.

Karen passed a bit later in the night without regaining consciousness, with Bert, both grandmas, and Grandpa McCarthy at her bedside. Grandpa called the hospice nurse and mortician. Grandma Hill asked if she should wake the kids, but Bert couldn't decide. Grandma McCarthy chose not to wake the kids. "Let's give them a few more hours of peace before the mourning begins."

Chapter 12

Karen observes a gradual lightening of the darkness and seems to see the silhouette of a person, then a face, smiling. "Shalom, Karen. Welcome to Paradise. I'm Nora, your great-grandaunt on your mother's side. I'm so glad to see you; I've been waiting for you."

"Am I dead? Is this Heaven? Are you a giant?" asks Karen.

"Yes and no, and no. Your body died, but you, Karen, that is your soul, lives on. And this is not Heaven; it's Paradise, a place of rest and nurture while we wait for Heaven. We'll all join the Almighty in Heaven soon, but this is our home for now. And what a home it is! But before we get to all that, there are a couple of people I want you to meet." Nora turns with Karen in her arms toward some folks standing around, anxiously awaiting their turn to welcome the soul home.

"This is your Aunt Martha and Uncle Joey. You never met them. But they watched you grow and took quite an interest in you." The couple nod and smile deeply. "Bless you, my child," they say.

"And this is Mr. Andres, the neighbor man from Philips Street who used to run you around in his wheelbarrow when you were just a toddler." He kisses her gently on the forehead.

"You know Grandfather Sam and your Grandmother Adeline on your mother's side." They kiss Karen and pronounce a short blessing and welcome.

"You never met Bill and Henrietta, your grandparents on your father's side," says Nora.

"We saw you a couple of times when you were just about as you are now, just a wee little one. We love you so, dear. Welcome home," they say.

"I'm so glad to meet you all, but why is everyone a giant?" asks Karen.

"We're not giants, child. But Karen, I've been given the honor of being your buddy. Everyone who first enters Paradise gets a buddy to help them learn the ropes, so to speak. Paradise is on a buddy system. You'll attend school for a while; I'll attend with you. Then you'll be free to do whatever you like."

"Attend school? What school? Whatever I like?"

An angel begins to appear. It's Angel Jaynes, who introduces himself as "Karen's angel."

"Blessings, child, and welcome to Paradise in The Name Above All Names. I will look after your ultimate welfare and spiritual development," said Angel Jaynes, "and you can call me AJ for short. You're an infant now, Karen. That's why everyone appears to be a giant. All people enter Paradise as 'spiritual infants,' but mature spiritually, gradually conforming to His Lordship's vision of them." AJ then picks Karen up and says a prayer, offering her to His Lordship. When he sets her down, she's about seven years old (Karen does not observe her instantaneous spiritual development).

"I want to go to school. When can I go?" exclaims Karen, jumping about while turning toward Nora.

"Right now, dear, I'll take you there."

"I can't accompany you now, ladies, and it seems I have a mission back on Earth. I bid you goodbye for now, and I'll catch up with you later," says AJ.

"An angel! AJ's an angel? I have my very own angel! (a brief moment of some smiles) What is an angel anyway?" Karen asks. "I don't feel any pain! I feel, I feel, good! I forgot what good feels like."

Chapter 13

Upon returning to the Hill's house, AJ detours and greets Angel Sarai. Sarai is now in the African savanna, ministering to wildebeests. "Greetings, Sarai!" exclaims AJ.

"Greetings in the joy of the Lord, Jaynes. Good to see you again so soon. Do you know what your new mission is yet?" asks Sarai.

"Yes. I've been given a social-working project with a human who just entered Paradise. I'm on my way to observe her biological family on Earth and just thought I'd take a moment and see how you're getting on without me," responds AJ.

"Don't flatter yourself, my friend. You know perfectly well I couldn't get along without you," says Sarai.

"Thanks, you're such an encouragement," AJ says.

"So, why are you really here? What's on your heart, Jaynes? Is it your new mission?"

"Yes. I've been assigned a human female as my charge. She just died and left a family behind. Of course, she has a husband, daughter, and son. I was there when she passed; she was comfortable, but her family will be grieving for some time. I fear this is a family of classic dysfunction; outcomes do not look promising," reports AJ.

"Sounds appropriate and interesting so far. What's the issue?" Sarai asks.

"I don't think I'm the angel for this. I've lived all these many centuries devoted to our great Lordship, His honor, and His will, serving, as you know, in many capacities and loving each one. But to be assigned the welfare of a human being is contrary to my nature."

"Then it's your dislike of human beings?" asks Sarai.

"Not dislike. I don't wish them any harm. It's just that I feel no love for them. I'm angry at them for denying and rejecting His Lordship. (a brief pause) The blaspheming of His Name from their lips is like the unending deluge over Niagara Falls," remarks AJ.

"All this is true, my friend. But you know our Lord's plan for man's redemption and absolute restoration. So, what's the real issue, Jaynes?"

"You just can't let well enough alone, can you? I should know by now that I can't hide anything from you—I would never think or do anything that would fail to fully honor His Lordship, and whatever work He has given me to do, I'll do. But I feel so distant from people. I'm afraid for the first time in my long life that I might fail Him," AJ says.

"Jaynes, it's not in your nature to fail Him. You can't, you won't. Stop worrying. I don't envy you this assignment with humans, but He'll provide you with whatever is needed to accomplish His will. You know that. And I don't think I need to tell you the obvious, do I?" asks Sarai.

"What's obvious?" asks AJ as he turns briefly away from Sarai. With hands raised, he pronounces, "Wait, silence, please! Listen to the great sage wisdom from the angel of the ages!"

"Stop being ridiculous. I'm serious, Jaynes. Our good King, God, and gracious Lord gave you this mission precisely because of your anger toward man. I can't wait to see you change! What a remarkable transformation it will be."

"You think you're so smart, don't you? I don't think that's it at all. You're way off base, and I'm quite sure there won't be any transformation. Now, if you'll pardon me, I've taken just about all the abuse an angel can handle in any given century; I'm off to my project."

"That's why I like you so much; you've got a great sense of human. I mean humor."

"That's not funny, Sarai."

Chapter 14

It's a Wednesday in the town of Little Hope, and Roy's in his second-period history class. It's been about two weeks since his mother passed. Life does not seem real to Roy; his home feels empty, with no joy, color, music, peace, comfort, or direction.

So, this is the sixth-grade class of Tulsa Jr. High—now, which one are you, Roy? AJ thinks to himself. "Ah, yes."

"Hey, twerp, I'm glad your mother's dead, one less twerp in Little Hope. I hope you're next," insults Barry the Ball-Buster. Without thinking, Roy throws his US History book at Barry, causing a considerable class disruption. Mrs. Tilton, whose back was previously turned to the students, spins around with shock and observes Roy threatening Barry.

"Tommy"—who was sitting next to Barry—"did you see what happened?" asks Mrs. Tilton as she hustles toward the commotion.

"Roy threw his book at Barry, Mrs. Tilton."

"Roy! Why did you throw your book at Barry?"

Roy can say nothing he's so angry and hurt, but Barry butts in, "He just threw it at me, Mrs. Tilton. For no reason!"

Mrs. Tilton asks the class, "Did anyone see what happened?" No one responds. The teacher scribbles a brief note, hands it to Roy, and summarily sends him to the principal's office while doting over Barry and sending him to the nurse's office escorted by Patty, one of the students. After Barry leaves the room, another student says, "Barry said some mean things to Roy, Mrs. Tilton."

"What things, Tim?" asks Mrs. Tilton.

"He said he's glad Roy's mom died," said Tim with a sniffle. Mrs. Tilton scribbles another note and has Tim bring it to the office as a follow-up to the previous one.

A few moments after taking a seat in the waiting area, the office administrator summons Roy to enter the vice principal's office, Mrs. Tilton's note preceding Roy by several minutes. "Roy Hill. What is this? Are you throwing your textbooks at a classmate? What on Earth could have motivated you to do such a thing?" asks the VP, Ms. Lumbar. Roy is unable to get any words out, not even with some gentle but firm coaxing. Then, like the cavalry finally arriving at the last minute, the second note is brought into the office, which Ms. Lumbar reads and, in one of those vice principal all-knowing postures, says softly, "I see."

Turning toward Roy, now understanding his hurt a bit better, she adds, "Roy, I know you're hurting terribly. Barry was wrong to say that to you. I'm so sorry. I'm going to have you speak with our school counselor, Mrs. Chatsworth. I believe she may be able to help you. Mrs. Jaymath, out in the office, will set up the appointment for you. Now you go back to class. Are you going to be alright? And no more book-throwing, young man, no matter what anyone else says. Do you understand?"

"Yes, ma'am," is said through a few tears and sniffles.

***

On the way home that day, Roy is walking kinda slow, head down, still reeling from the earlier event, when he hears, "Hey, twerp! Thought you could get away with diss'n me, eh? Time for a lesson!" AJ sees the shadow of a figure whispering to three boys, making a straight line toward him.

Barry and two of his buddies push Roy around, and Barry socks him in the eye and stomach, then leaves him with a warning: "This ain't nothing compared to what you'll get if you rat on us. Understand, twerp?"

I don't want to live anymore. God, why didn't you take me too when you took my mom? Nobody loves me anymore, and I don't love anyone; I want to go to Heaven and be with my mom, Roy prays.

AJ walks over close to Roy, kneels, and calmly says: "This is not God's will for you, Roy. Those boys are being influenced by evil to torment you. Evil wants your soul, Roy, but it can't have it. His Lordship has called you His own." Roy can't hear AJ with his ears, but he does perceive a bit of comfort in the midst of his abuse.

Roy cries on the ground for a moment, wipes his nose and tears carefully ('cause his eye stings), slowly gets up, picks up his books, and resumes his walk home. When he arrives, Roy races into the house, slams the front door, and flies into his room, slamming that door, too. He cries in his room, angry at God for his beating and for the injustice he endured in class, but mostly for his mom's sickness and death. Roy's thoughts of remorse revolve around the fact that *she was the only one who loved me; she took care of me, and now she's gone forever, and it's your fault, God.* AJ remains near Roy and continues to speak healing and comfort to him during this grim hour: "Don't dwell on your pain. Forgive them, Roy. Your mother's well, I promise you. This will be a long process, Roy, and I'll be with you each step of the way, child."

After a while, Roy composes himself a bit and starts to do his chores (taking out the trash). He does it in the bathrooms, but before he can get to it in the kitchen, Melody, who is taking out one of the frozen dinners provided by the church while silently complaining that *it's another casserole!* says to Roy, "Dinner will be ready in forty minutes."

"Thank you for making dinner, Melody," Roy says. She yells at Roy for calling her Melody—her name from now on is "Crescenda, you retard!" But then she notices Roy's bruised eye and feels sympathy for the first time in weeks. "What happened to you? Come here; let me put some ice on it."

"Nothing. Just some bullies being jerks."

"Here, put this on. Leave it on for five minutes, and do it as often as you can tonight. Sit down for a few minutes and let the ice work." Roy gratefully accepts the wrapped ice and cooperatively situates it on his face. He hasn't been nurtured by a soul since well before his mom's death, and it feels good.

Melody just put the church dinner in the oven when Bert comes home. "Melody, I'm home. When's dinner?" AJ observes a shadow accompanying Bert as he enters his home; the shadow speaks to Bert: "I'm hungry! Where's my food? Why don't I get any respect around here?" and the like.

"Not too long; I'm putting it in the oven now. Maybe thirty minutes?"

"Thirty minutes! Listen, I come home hungry after a long day's work, and I want dinner ready on time when I get home—"

"I'm sorry. I had extra homework, and I'm just a little late." *Not too bad,* she thinks to herself. Indeed, he's been home almost a minute, and there's been a minimum of conflict and yelling. Bert picks up the day's mail, thumbs through cursing and pitching bills as he heads over to his easy chair and plops in, fingers the remote, and channel surfs while impatiently waiting for his meal. Bert drinks a double.

"It's in the oven now. It was really frozen solid. It shouldn't be too long," she says as she turns up the heat to 450 and gives Roy a wink. Roy's heart surges as he thinks about the possibility that Melody might like him and that maybe they can be a family after all (at least he and Melody), but then plummets as he contemplates losing that, too.

AJ observes the shadow now move toward Melody, and it starts to speak to her: "I hate this. I have to do everything around here. Nobody ever helps me. Family? What family? This family is a joke—"

After several minutes, Bert yells at Melody: "Do I smell something burning? What are you do'n with my dinner?" The oven is a little hot and hasn't been cleaned for at least four years, so it's smelling up the kitchen just a bit. Melody takes the half-frozen casserole from the oven, dishes some on a plate for Bert, and pops it into the microwave. *Good think'n, girl,* she says to herself as she prepares to serve him in his recliner in front of the TV.

AJ observes the shadow follow Melody into the living room as she brings Bert his supper. It speaks to both of them simultaneously, and their demeanors sour. Melody tells her dad she needs money as she delivers dinner to his recliner: "I need some money."

"Money! What for? For crying out loud!"

"Female stuff. OK?"

"Don't you already have all that? How much do you need?"

"$30."

"$30! For what? I ain't giving you $30!"

"Alright, then $20. OK?"

"I'll give you $10; you better make it last. My wallet's over on the table. Bring it to me."

Melody neglects to dish up Roy's dinner, allowing him to fend for himself. She takes her plate, goes into her room, and talks to one friend after another—playing the good daughter and good sister.

When Bert gets up after dinner to throw his tray and dishes into the sink, he observes the trash overflowing and stinking. He yells for Roy and slaps him on the head. Roy completes his chores, then undertakes his hygiene regiment and goes to bed, lost and so alone, but he manages to pray before bed. "God, please forgive me for yelling at you earlier today. And for forgetting to do my chores. And for being such a loser. And please take good care of my mom."

AJ observes the shadow approach Roy. It tries to say something, but Roy isn't influenced in the least. AJ then addresses the evil spirit and bids it, "Leave Roy alone; he doesn't belong to your master." And the shadow leaves, for now.

AJ departs from Roy and returns to the ladies in Paradise, walking toward the Belush'ya Young Souls School.

Chapter 15

The ladies are walking along a bustling thoroughfare, engaged in conversation, when AJ appears. "May you always find grace in the presence of the Almighty," AJ blesses as he greets them. They're walking on a grass-covered section of a large boulevard. Various vibrantly colored wildflowers grow singly and in clusters from the grass. Their petals sing a soft resonance coaxed by the gentle breeze, and their varied fragrances rise like a whisper. A majestic canopy of forestation provides an overhead dimension of structural beauty.

"There must be thousands of souls on the boulevard," remarks Karen. Some folks are navigating toward a destination, some standing still, many singing and dancing, many praying, others worshipping and giving thanks. There's no conflict or disharmony of any kind, just peace and beauty, thankfulness and purpose. *I've never seen people so happy. And all getting along; and so clean! And such a clean environment,* Karen thinks to herself through tears of joy.

"It's this way in every city, town, and village in Paradise. This is such a wonderful place; it's almost impossible to imagine that Heaven could be any better," Nora says.

"Ah, but it is. You're in for such a treat!" responds AJ.

"Hi, AJ. Welcome back," says Nora.

"What are all these art deco and ultra-modern buildings? They all have street-level shops, stores, and what appear to be office fronts," asks Karen.

"We're at the heart of Belush'ya, Paradise's most modern city. It's where believers first enter Paradise. And this downtown is much like what one might expect to see in a city on Earth, except everything is pure and clean, and the only signage appears to be carved wood, engraved metal, or precious stone," answers Nora.

Karen turns toward Nora and asks if she died young. "No, I was seventy-six years old," Nora responds. Karen asks why she's so young now. "Because this is my spiritual age. We do not yet have bodies, but we are congruent souls and operate in the spiritual domain, which we call Paradise." Karen asks how old Nora is. "It's not important. Whatever age we are, we need only be faithful to His Lordship and each other. We each progress spiritually at our own pace. His Lordship doesn't mind if we mature slowly; neither is he more delighted in us if we progress quickly. The Holy One loves us, each of us deeply, and His Lordship permits us to develop at whatever pace we are comfortable with."

"Can I see myself in a mirror, Nora?" Karen asks.

Nora responds, "There are no mirrors in Paradise, but if you look deeply into AJ's face, he can reflect your and other images too."

"Wow. You can do that, AJ?"

"Yes. But we'll save that for the proper time."

The trio makes its way through a quaint section of Belush'ya, called Greenwich Village, to an enormous meadow referred to by the locals as Central Park. Greenwich Village opens up into a plaza. At the far end of the plaza are gates to Central Park. The gates are huge in size but inviting in beauty as if beckoning to show us more. No walls encompass the park, but multiple roads from different parts of the city lead to the gate. AJ tells Karen, "There are twelve such gates that comprise Central Park's portals, which house the school. This gate is called Believer's Gate."

From a great distance, they can see a large, gently sloping hill in the center of the meadow, and people are gathered around. Many thousands, perhaps tens of thousands, of souls clustered like pepper flakes over the visible expanse of the hill. Young and old. All are conversing politely; no one is isolated or shunned; there is much laughter, smiling, songs, worshipping His Lordship, mini-lectures, and discussions. AJ interrupts and blesses Nora and Karen, then politely excuses himself to return to Earth to revisit the Hill family.

Chapter 16

It's about one Earth week since AJ's last visit—a Thursday evening. Melody is in her room speaking with one of her friends when Derek texts in. She breaks her call and calls Derek back—they speak for a long time. Bert (after several drinks) yells to Melody to "stop yapp'n on the phone, get to bed. And get your darn light off." Derek tells Melody to sneak out of the house and meet him at the corner. She agrees, and they spend the night together. She sneaks back into the house before Bert gets up and before Roy gets up to go to school.

The next day, she skips school to hang out at the mall. When she's at school, she skips classes to hang out in the girls' bathroom. Bert's being sent notices from school, but Melody throws them away and deletes them from V-mail before Bert gets home. Her senior year is a wreck; she's gonna fail, but she doesn't need school. She has Derek!

It's a Tuesday evening. Bert is out at Finnegan's Pub, reinforcing his manhood. When the doorbell rings, Melody is having a rare moment of bonding time with Roy, watching "Vampire something or other" on TV.

"Hello. We're Chris and Natalie Hergaard. We're on the Visitation Team from church. We've stopped over to bring you another couple of frozen dinners."

"Thanks for the food. My dad's not home yet." She does not invite them in.

They ask if the family will attend church next Sunday. "Please do and sit with us during service. We could even stop by and pick you all up in the church van."

Melody responds, "Sure, thanks," and hurries them off, but before she can shut the door, Roy hears the conversation (as a commercial's on and he's coming out of the living room). "I'll come to church this Sunday. I usually walk. Can you pick us up? Sometimes my dad has a headache in the morning and doesn't want to drive. Last week, I had to walk in the rain."

"You poor dear, yes, of course. We'll be here at 8:45 a.m. Looking forward to seeing you all. Goodbye, and have a good night."

***

On Sunday morning, the doorbell rings, and Roy answers. He's the only one up, and he's as dressed for church as he can be (clothes are mostly clean but pretty wrinkled). Bert's asleep still hungover, and Melody's not home yet (though no one knows it; she snuck out last evening again to spend the night partying). Roy spends Sunday mornings in the youth group; they feed the kids some juice and a few snacks, for which Roy is grateful since he did not have any breakfast. When Roy returns from church, Melody is home, but she's in her room with her door closed, and Bert is sick in the bathroom.

***

The next day, as soon as Bert returns home from the office, with the vexing shadow (now revealing more form) at his side, the phone rings. Having mail and keys in his hands, Bert is clumsily looking around for somewhere to set stuff aside as he answers the phone. AJ hears the silhouette speaking to Bert: "Can't I have five minutes' peace? Do they have to start ragging on me the second I walk through the door?"

"So glad I'm finally able to reach you, Bert. Sorry, this is Pastor Bilford. We haven't seen you and the kids at church for such a long time. That is, except Roy. I think he's been coming pretty regular. Anyway, I'm concerned about you; we all are. How are you getting on?"

"Oh. Hello, Pastor Bilford. I'm getting on just fine (said in a terse manner). Been so busy, you know, with the kids and work. They're killing me at work with OT. I'm used to the single-parent thing, but it's pretty tough sometimes," Bert says.

"Is there anything you need? I understand Mrs. Fowles has organized some of the ladies to deliver dinners to you and the kids. Are they all right? Do you have enough?" Pastor Bilford asks.

"Oh yeah, they're pretty good. And I think we still have plenty. It's about the only good food any of us get anymore." AJ observes the silhouette speaking non-stop directly at Bert, who is increasingly agitated.

"That's good. We care about you and the kids, Bert. I hope you know that. I know how hard it is to lose a wife and a mother," says the pastor.

"Have you lost a wife? No, I don't think so, and you don't know how I feel, alright?" Bert asks sarcastically.

"You're right, Bert, I'm sorry. I haven't lost my wife, and I don't know exactly how you feel. But I have suffered alongside many good folks who have lost a spouse. And I'm concerned that you're blaming God. Is that why you're not coming to church, Bert?" AJ observes that the silhouette is speaking louder and more aggressively, evoking more anger in Bert. AJ tries to speak peace to Bert, but Bert doesn't perceive goodness, peace, or healing; he only perceives anger, victimhood, and his own pain.

"No, I don't—yes, I do blame God. Who else? I slaved all these years, working for my family, trying to get ahead, then Karen got sick, and I lost ten years of my life caring for her and raising kids that don't give a darn. She left me with thirty thousand dollars' worth of medical bills! You bet I'm angry at God! What did I ever do to deserve this? Never mind, you don't have the answer, but I do! I didn't do anything to deserve this! So, either your God is unjust or doesn't even exist. I'm so through with your God and your church. And you can tell your precious church ladies to keep their crummy dinners!" Slam goes the phone. Bert hits the open bottle.

A bit later that evening, Bert's dinner will be interrupted by another unwanted phone call. Unfortunately for the caller, Bert's already got a few drinks under his belt. AJ observes that the silhouette has been nagging Bert non-stop for over an hour. The silhouette yells at Bert: "That darn woman left me with a federal debt in medical bills! She never really loved me! She never even appreciated me! I slaved away the best years of my life for her! For what? To be left with forty thousand dollars in medical bills!"

The phone rings, and Bert answers, "Hello. Who the heck is this now, calling at the dinner hour?"

"I'm sorry for bothering you and disturbing your dinner. I'm Dr. Gregory, looking for Mr. Hill. But this must be a bad time—"

"Oh, sorry, Doc. I thought you were a bill collector or that darn pastor from the church bothering me again."

"I'm happy to call back at a better time, Mr. Hill. I was just thinking about you and wanted to check in. How are you getting on?"

"Well, how do you think I am? I'm dying here. Karen, darn her, left me with over fifty thousand dollars in medical bills, and she spoiled those kids so rotten I can't do anything with 'em. I'm dying over here, but I'm done sacrificing my life for everybody else. I'm gonna finally start to think about me and do what I wanna do—"

"Well, that's good, Mr. Hill. You should get some rest and try to reduce your stress—"

"Oh heck, don't go into all that. You don't know noth'n about stress! I know 'bout stress! You don't know noth'n!"

"I'm sorry to have bothered you, Mr. Hill. I can see this is a bad time for you. Please forgive me. Goodbye."

"Yeah, well, up yours, *doctor don't know noth'n 'bout no stress*!"

AJ's hurt and dejected over being unable to draw Bert toward God, spiritual health, or light. AJ leaves the Hill's house and returns to Paradise.

Chapter 17

AJ returns to visit briefly with Angel Sarai. "Greetings, Sarai."

"Greetings, Jaynes. What's wrong? Your face betrays you."

"I hoped to gain some insight and feeling for man from my observations of my project's family, but it is just terrible, worse than I could have imagined. They are vile and base and so susceptible to evil's influence," complains AJ.

"I'm sorry for your burden, Jaynes. But if the Lord has given you this mission, there must be a reason. I wish I could help you bear it," Sarai says.

"You help by listening and offering wisdom and encouragement, my friend."

AJ then returns to the plaza before the great meadow and appears to the ladies as they briefly hang over the rail on a bridge spanning a crystal-clear brook, looking into the water at the fish leisurely swimming by. People of all sizes, ages, and types travel in both directions on the beautifully carved wooden footbridge; after all, Belush'ya is a city of about 700 million souls and Greenwich Village is home to about 50 million—mostly teachers, singers, artists, musicians, and artsy folks, people bent toward subjective and creative occupations.

Karen sees an infant in the arms of his buddy, walking in the same direction as them, coming toward them, and asks about the baby. AJ explains that he was: "An eighty-seven-year-old man when he died. He had come to Christ early in adulthood but failed to abide in the

Lord while living, so he never developed spiritually very much. He served as an elder in his church yet never attained spiritual maturity. In contrast, you are about eight years old now, Karen.

"But as you can see, most students attending school are babies or children; you're one of the eldest students here. That's because you've matured spiritually quite a bit while making your way toward school. I don't think you'll be in school very long."

AJ says that there are perhaps ten such schools in Paradise, all operating concurrently. AJ further explains that a person's or angel's spiritual maturity is proportional to a person's intimacy in a healthy relationship with His Lordship. As they grow closer to The Holy One, they are increasingly transformed into the image of His Son.

The trio continues their trek in the direction of the school. The street is immaculately clean, as is everything in Paradise. The Believer's Gate is immense, architected as two enormous towers spanned by an arch. On the arch are hundreds of large, colorful banners representing every tribe and tongue of man. At the base of the gate, three roads converge from different areas of the plaza, and greeting committees welcome the souls entering the park.

Beyond the gate, a dense forest of mixed coniferous and deciduous growth explodes. A wide and winding road enters the Deborah Forest from the gate. Most people are traveling either one way or the other on the road, although some folks are seen in the forest enjoying nature the Almighty created. As the trio passes a bend in the road, they see a rather large group of people enjoying a concert given by a boy about Karen's age playing the guitar. The boy is singing about His Lordship's goodness, the wonder of love, and the beauty of His Lordship's creation—the mountains, the forest, the oceans, and all the living creatures. His voice is remarkably melodic and strong, and the trio can hear him pretty clearly, even from a distance. They stop and listen for a while, and then Karen comments, "His music is so beautiful and positive. He seems strangely familiar to me. I think I know him."

"I'm sure you do," AJ responds. "John was a very popular musician during your younger years on Earth. He had lots of ups and downs. JD lost his way more than once but reached out to His Lordship in the end. And now he worships His Lordship faithfully at every moment, offering wonderful songs of praise and thanksgiving here in Paradise. I believe his name on Earth was John Denver."

"John Denver! Yes, of course. I recognize him. That is, I recognize his music. How wonderful," Karen adds.

"Yes, it is wonderful. And it's equally wonderful in the case of every soul that is saved. It's an expression of His Lordship's overwhelming goodness toward human souls," responds AJ. And the three say in unison, "Amen."

The trio continues along the road and enters a clearing characteristic of an alpine meadow with a lush carpet of green grass seasoned with abundant wildflowers of every known and unknown variety, aroma, and color. In the approximate center of the expansive meadow is a large hill, almost a mountain. Tens of thousands of folks are on the slope, listening, organized into many small groups. Karen imagines that *this must be the school, and these must be the student*s.

People and angels take turns teaching in each of the small groups. There are no breaks; none are needed. No one is tired or bored; even little ones understand.

The ladies perceive beautiful music, wonderful aromas, breathtaking sights, and even the words that are taught sound like song—healing, strengthening, and life-giving song. Teaching is sometimes interrupted by spontaneous thanksgiving and worship. Karen asks her companions, "What is being taught, and what do the students learn?"

"An interesting and advanced understanding, Karen," AJ responds. "Many times in human life, what's being taught is not what's being learned. But in this case, these are synonymous. I believe you humans have a saying that goes something like this: 'The most important lessons are caught, not taught.' This is a true saying, especially here. And the students are literally being transformed into spiritual maturity, not as much by cognitive advancement as much as by relational advancement."

"What do you mean relational advancement, AJ?" asks Karen.

"Maturing of the heart, more than the head. People are very smart, but relationally, people are very primitive, doing all manners of grotesque evil to one another, to strangers, to loved ones. There is no limit to the boundless evil that man perpetrates on man. His Lordship does not focus on the development of your minds in Paradise as much as your hearts," AJ continues.

"I see. This makes sense," Karen responds—a brief pause of silence.

"You asked what topics are being taught. Here's a list." AJ hands Karen a scroll. Karen reads:

The Belush'ya School of Young Souls

Praise The NAME Above All Names

Young Soul's Syllabus

- Theology- Who His Lordship is (His names, nature, and love)
- Soteriology- Who you are in His Lordship (His adopted child)
- Exegesis- Explanation of scriptures and doctrines
- Hermeneutics I- Personal freedoms & options
- Hermeneutics II- Roles and responsibilities

- Hierarchy in Heaven and Paradise
- Spiritual maturation process and eventual mission
- Eschatology- Heaven! Christ the King! The Bride of Christ!
- Protocol when in His Lordship's presence (very serious, much prayer before teaching, much devotion in teaching and learning)

"The way it works is that new students enter a newly formed class, then students progress from class to class near the base of the hill and proceed to more advanced classes up the hill. Finally, the students reach the class at the pinnacle; once they pass their final exams, they graduate!" AJ says.

"This is wonderful. I can't wait to start," says Karen.

"You don't have to wait. There, to the right, is a brand-new class forming. Go take your place," AJ instructs, and Karen bolts off in an all-out sprint toward the group of students assembling.

"Wait, wait for me! I'm Karen—"

It appears that about a hundred students and ten to twelve teachers—roughly half the teachers are people, the others are angels—comprise the new class. AJ bids Nora goodbye for now, and Nora walks toward the new class to rejoin Karen.

AJ returns to Earth, this time back to Roy's sixth-grade math class.

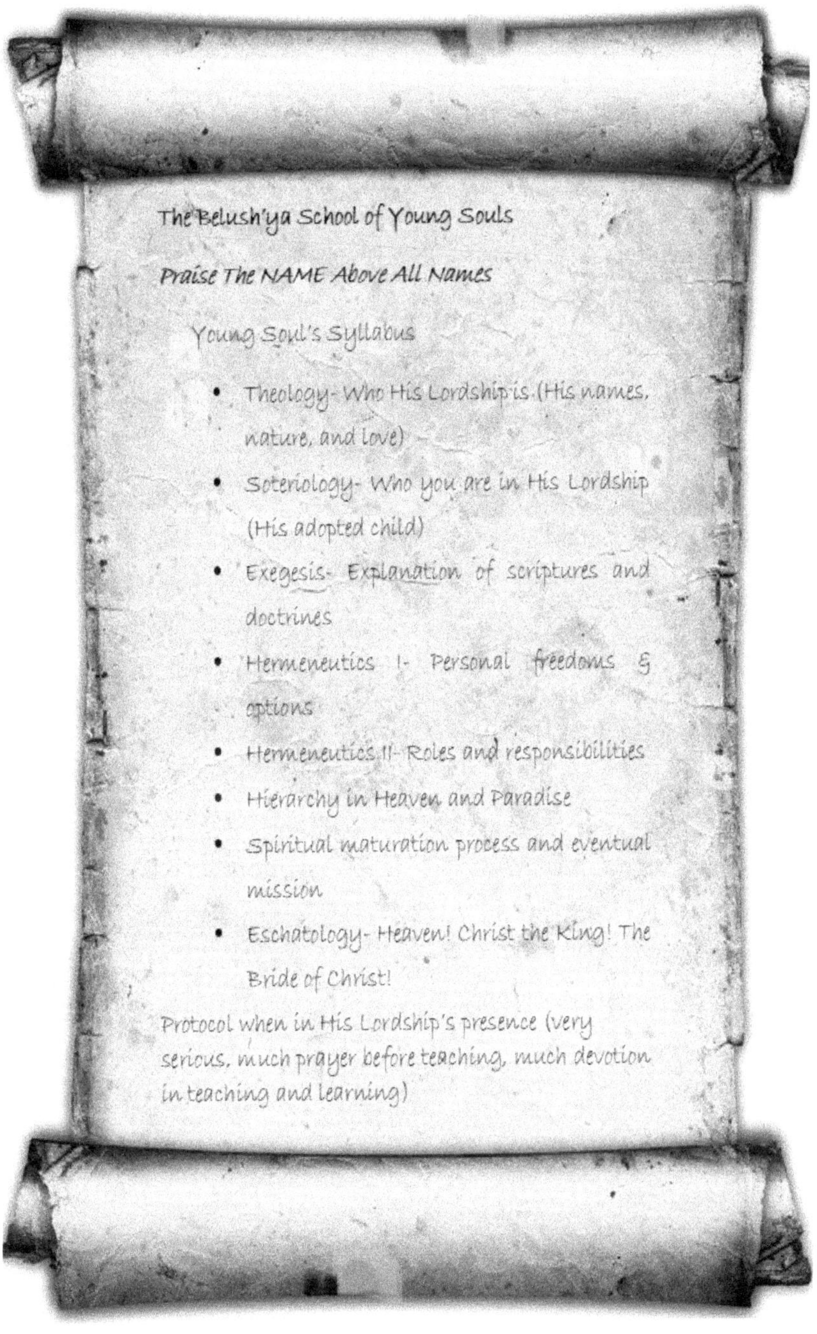

Figure 1 The Belush'ya School for Young Souls Scroll

Chapter 18

Roy is in class and gets a summons to Mrs. Chatsworth's office for their first consultation (it's about three days since the incident with Barry). He's excused from class by the math teacher and proceeds down the hall to the counselor's office. "Hello, Roy. I'm Mrs. Chatsworth. I understand your mother recently died. Can you tell me about it?"

"My mom had a heart condition, and she died."

"I know. Please tell me about how it happened. How did you feel during the time she was sick and then when she passed?"

"I really miss her. She was sick for a long time and couldn't do very much (tears start to well deep in Roy's eyes). She couldn't play or make meals or clean the house or anything. But she did try to sing to me sometime."

"Did she have a nice voice?"

"The prettiest voice in the world." Tears start to flow. "She would sing to me because Melody would sometimes treat me mean. And my dad would sometimes yell at me. It was all she could do."

"Who's Melody?"

"She's my oldest sister."

"Do you have other sisters or brothers?"

"No, just Melody. She's my oldest sister."

"Your mother's singing must have been a comfort to you. How do you get some comfort now?"

"I don't know," Roy responds, shrugging his shoulders.

"Who comforts you now?" Just silence. "Does your sister sing to you?"

"No. She doesn't even like me. She hates me," Roy says.

"Of course she doesn't hate you, Roy. She's your sister. She's grieving too. She's in pain too. Give her some time." Silence. "How does your dad comfort you?" Silence again. "Does your dad talk to you about your feelings?" asks Ms. Chatsworth.

"No. He doesn't talk to me; he only yells," says Roy.

"Did you have a favorite song that your mother sang to you?" asks Ms. Chatsworth.

"*Born Free* was my favorite," responds Roy. "Sometimes I can hear her sing it, and it makes me cry."

"Oh, that's one of my favorites too," says the counselor. "I cry when I hear it. It seems like we have a lot in common, Roy. Our time's about over today. It was my pleasure making your acquaintance. We'll meet again next week; I look forward to it."

***

The counselor wrote session notes for about ten minutes and decided that Roy might benefit from talking to Coach Binder, the football coach. Ms. Chatsworth brought up the idea in their next session. Roy didn't seem too interested in talking with the coach, but he was intrigued by the prospect of football and consented to meet with him.

AJ accompanied Roy home from school and watched over him that evening (as he had many times before).

***

The next day, AJ decided to accompany Bert to work.

As it approached 10 a.m., Bert and several office mates got ready to break for coffee. "Hey, buddy, you've been real down ever since … you know. Well, I know what you need. You sacrificed for your wife,

65

but now she's gone, and you've gotta live your life. Let me fix you up. We could double date. My girl told me about one of her friends that's just become available. She's hot! Whittaya think?" asks one of Bert's buddies.

"Yeah, maybe you're right. I've spent the last fifteen years sacrificing my life for that darn woman. She left me with a hundred thousand in medical bills and two spoiled brats. She ruined those darn kids; I had them well-mannered, and she made 'em lazy and good for noth'n—" complains Bert.

"Hey, man, enough about all that! You just need what a good woman can give. Hear what I'm saying?" says Bert's friend.

"Yeah, man, you're right. What's this woman's name?" asks Bert.

"I don't remember, man. What the heck does that matter anyway? She's a woman, know what I mean

"Heck yes, I know what you mean. Man, it's been like ten years. Yeah, I'm ready. I wanna meet this woman," Bert says.

"Betty says we should double date for the first date. I don't know. Are you okay with that, buddy?" asks the friend.

"Sure, I guess. I'm okay with a double date. When are we going?"

"I'll talk to Betty and set it up. Now cheer up, man. Life's gonna get good real soon. You know what I'm talk'n 'bout!" says Bert's friend.

"Man. You're a good friend. Not like those hypocrites at church—" Bert says.

***

Later that week, the double-date arrangements were made. Bert met his friend Wayne and the ladies, Betty and Margareta, at a local restaurant for dinner. The original shadow speaking to Bert several weeks ago had recently become a silhouette, but now the silhouette seemed more substantial than AJ had previously observed. It spoke all manner of self-indulgence to Bert: "I need this, I deserve this, this is me-time…" Margareta had her own shadow speaking to her. The evil spirits tag-teamed, continuously speaking justification of self-gratification to both of them.

AJ again tried to intervene and speak repentance to each of them but to no avail. The demons rebuffed AJ. "This one's mine," said Bert's silhouette, and "This one belongs to my master," said Margareta's shadow.

It was pretty uneasy at first, but after a few drinks, Bert and Margareta were hitting it off. Bert exaggerated his financial stability, and Margareta feigned more purity and piety than appropriate for a woman of her experience. As the dinner ended, Bert and Margareta indicated that Wayne and Betty should probably head home: "It's a workday tomorrow." Wayne was all for it, but Betty asked Margareta if she was absolutely sure. She was, and within five minutes of the friends' exit, the new couple was heading to Margareta's apartment. *Heck, the kids can take care of themselves. I've provided everything they need, and this is for me; I deserve it,* Bert says to himself.

Chapter 19

AJ returns to Paradise and stops to see Angel Sarai before returning to the ladies. "Sarai, I'm so angry at people throwing their lives away. They don't seem to recognize their human value, the value The Holy One gives to each life He creates."

"Well, that's a step up, Jaynes. At least you're recognizing that even man has some value, even if only as a primitive life form. Tell me, what's going on that has you so burdened?"

"I've just observed a man, my case's former husband, who is throwing his life and the lives of his children away. His kids struggle to survive, and he's so preoccupied with his own pain and self-interests that he doesn't even notice his children are prey for evil, never mind their human needs for safety, love, and nurturing," AJ laments.

"I'm distressed to hear of their self-inflicted misfortune. How can I help? Can I pray for them and you?" asks Angel Sarai.

"Yes, please, Sarai. Pray for us. Pray that the Almighty will intervene and reach Bert, Melody, and Roy before it's too late. Pray that His Lordship will help me and give me wisdom and skill to minister to my family, that is, my case's family."

"Dear Lord, our Lord, most holy and compassionate, please intervene on behalf of Jaynes and his family. Within the bounds of Your will, we pray for the rescue, redemption, and restoration of these souls. And thank You for beginning to open our eyes and hearts to Your love of man."

"Amen" is said in unison.

"Thanks, Sarai," AJ says. "But what did you mean about 'my family'?"

"You said it first, brother. I was just praying in agreement with you," responds Sarai.

"Yeah, but I didn't mean exactly that. I was just at a loss for words and got tongue-tied," AJ says.

"Yes, of course," Sarai says, "I often get tongue-tied myself. I know the feeling."

AJ rejoins the ladies at school. Karen's soaking up everything. She appears to be about eleven years old and is ready to graduate. Graduation parties are optional, and Karen's too excited to slow down for a party; she wants to commence practicing what she's been taught. The graduation ceremony is rather brief but somewhat elaborate. High-ranking elders and angels congratulate the graduates and confer upon them their Tribal and Angelic Family positions and robes. Karen is informed that she's of the Tribe of Naftali, the Family of the Archangel Chamuel, and the city of Servern'ya. Her mission is servanthood, and her occupation is whatever she pleases.

Karen's told that her course through school was equivalent to about two Earth weeks. Nora tells Karen that she's one of the quickest learners she's seen. "You know, it's mostly girls who are initially faster learners for some reason; boys start out slower—but then they never do catch up," says Nora as they both enjoy a good laugh.

The trio meanders down the well-worn path from the class to a lovely area in the great meadow by a pond to reflect and discuss the next steps. "Folks often travel to their home cities to take up an apprenticeship, to learn their mission, and develop their skills and maturity. Sometimes, people travel to various places in Paradise to meet people, see interesting places, and enjoy exciting experiences. And some people just play games," explains Nora.

"Games? What kind of games?" asks Karen.

"Any and every kind of game you can think of. Soccer, golf, football, baseball—"

"Baseball?"

"Sure. Baseball's very popular in Paradise. There are many, many teams. I've seen a few games myself," says Nora.

"And we can go watch some games? How do we pay for the tickets?"

"There are no tickets. Everything's free in Paradise. And you can not only watch as many games as you like, but you can play yourself," Nora says.

"I could play baseball? Real baseball? On a real team?"

"You bet. Real baseball on a real team," AJ says.

"Sure, like Little League, right?"

"No, ma'am, like real professional baseball," says AJ.

"No way! Are you sure this isn't Heaven? I wanta play baseball!"

"Okay, then it's set. Nora will escort you to join a team to play baseball," says AJ.

AJ blesses the ladies and returns to Earth again.

Chapter 20

Several weeks later, at the Hill house, Melody has no real appetite as she returns home from the mall (cutting class again). She's throwing up in the bathroom. As soon as she gets a break from the nausea, she's back on the phone with her friends. "I hate my loser family!" she protests.

"They're losers, all right, but you don't really hate 'em, girl. You just need your space, so they'll stop drag'n you down," responds the other girl on the phone.

"I do hate them. My dad's such a jerk, and my brother's a retard!" And so goes the endless procession of tirades, chats, and texting.

She's not eating again tonight but talking on the phone with her friends; they tell her she may be pregnant. She starts getting sick again.

***

The next day, Melody buys an OTC pregnancy test kit. She brings it home and hides it under her mattress. Later that evening, she goes into the bathroom and discovers that she's pregnant. At first, she's overjoyed, then terrified. She begins a deluge of texting and phone conversations. Some of her friends advise her to have an abortion. Some of her friends advise her to have the baby and go on welfare. Some of her friends urge her to run away with Derek. She decides on the last option; after all, they love each other and will be together forever. Melody calls Derek and says she desperately wants to see him, so they plan to meet down the street later that night after everyone's asleep. Derek's clueless about the nature of Melody's request; he thinks she's interested in having sex, so he's in.

Melody sneaks out of the house, and Derek's car waits for her down the block. Melody expresses her deep love and commitment, then transitions to say her brother and dad drive her crazy, and she wants to move in with him. Derek protests, "What the heck is all this complaining crap? I thought you wanted sex! I didn't come across town to listen to your problems."

Melody starts to cry. Derek gets angry, then calms down a bit. "Look. I'm sorry, okay? Now, just stop crying, all right? I know your dad's a jerk. What do you want me to do about it?" asks Derek.

"We could live together," responds Melody. "I want to be with you."

Derek's frustration is immediately triggered, but then he thinks about it. *Maybe it could work if she gets a job to help pay the bills.* Derek's been having a problem making ends meet lately; he's had to borrow money from friends just to keep a bit of gas in the car. "Okay, Melody," Derek says. "Let's give it a go."

Believing this was tantamount to a proposal, Melody agrees to move in and get a part-time job but says she wants to finish high school—she has only one semester remaining. Derek doesn't see the advantage in that, but he agrees.

The kids make their plans. Derek expresses that he doesn't want any trouble with her dad. Melody says there won't be any. She plans to leave a note and just disappear. "He won't even notice I'm gone."

So, with what Melody thinks is some clever investigative work over the next several days, she discovers when her dad is next planning to go on a date. "That's the night I'll run away." She doesn't have much to pack, mostly clothes and toiletries, and no room for most of her keepsakes, which she no longer wants anyway (including a long-necked plush giraffe named Margret Thatcher that her mother gave her when she got her first period).

Their plan is to distract Roy with a rented movie and then sneak Melody and her possessions out of the house before her dad returns from his date. The plan mostly works, except Roy notices the noise and investigates. At first, Roy's worried and concerned for Melody, but Derek assures Roy that everything's all right and asks Roy to help him put Melody's stuff in his car. Melody tells Roy not to tell Dad tonight. She tells Roy she's leaving Dad a note and that he'll see it in the morning, which will be soon enough. Once Melody is packed up, she gives Roy a candy bar and sends him to bed. Derek drives the two to his apartment to begin their lives together.

***

Roy's next few weeks at school were rather uneventful. He hoped to receive an invitation from his coach to play star quarterback, but his anticipation devolved into disappointment. His life at home was likewise uneventful since Melody was gone, and Bert was obsessed with Margareta. He tended to remain mostly alone—so as long as he did his chores and didn't draw any attention to himself, he was pretty much okay. Things seemed pretty quiet in his relationship with God, too. He'd pray every night and hoped that God took good care of his mother, but he had no discernible confirmation or assurance. Roy did receive a measure of acceptance and nurturing at the church youth group. And Mrs. Tilton was a bit more gentle and compassionate, so life was at least not getting any worse for Roy, for the moment anyway.

Part Three

Original Missourian

Chapter 21

Karen's so eager about baseball prospects that she's forgotten the beautiful sights, sounds, and aromas. "Which team?" asks Karen.

"We have about a hundred baseball teams in Paradise. Let's try the first team we come across," responds AJ.

"You mean, I just join the first team we come across?" asks Karen.

"Yes, you can join any team you wish, play for as long as you wish, and leave when you wish," responds AJ.

"What if the team doesn't have enough players to man a game?" Karen asks.

"Not to worry; a player from another team will join. There are no limitations or restrictions. We don't play baseball in Paradise like you played it on Earth. Baseball is not competitive as much as it is cooperative. Teams cheer for each other, and the goal is to encourage and reinforce the value of your fellow players regardless of their position, team, or skill level."

"This is unbelievable. It's so beautiful, but how can you play baseball like that? What does a game look like?"

AJ responds: "It looks like a young physician who loved baseball and was paralyzed from a broken neck due to a traffic accident, divorced by his wife, never visited by his children, and who rotted away in a convalescent home, but the one thing his damaged brain could remember and get out was the song 'Take Me Out to the Ball Game.' He loved baseball. When he got upset and agitated, which was quite frequent because he understood what happened to him and that his condition on Earth was hopeless, the nursing staff would start singing that song, and immediately, his demeanor would change; for a few moments, every now and then, he was happy. And now he's here in Paradise, playing ball, and playing ball, and playing ball! He's played every position many times, and he continues to play ball; in fact, he never has to stop playing ball until he decides to. You'll meet him; he's playing on your team."

"My team? Wow! I'd love to meet him. His life was so sad, but now it's full of joy. However, I don't understand how baseball is like his story."

"In Paradise, baseball, and everything, is cooperative. Bill couldn't play baseball on Earth anymore after his accident due to physical limitations, but he could in Paradise. In Paradise, Bill doesn't have any limitations. No one does. In Paradise, it's all about God and each other. We're family; we are healthy; we encourage each other to spiritual maturity through baseball, study, and any activity or inactivity. It all brings us closer to God. And God enjoys our enjoyment. He cries tears of joy as we take pleasure in Paradise." AJ pauses momentarily and then continues, "It's time, Karen, to look deep into my face."

After a few seconds, Karen sees her own face as a reflection in AJ's face, then responds, "Oh my." In a few more seconds, Karen says, "What's this? A person sitting in a wheelchair."

"This is Bill," AJ says. "I see what you see, or more accurately, you see what I see. I witnessed this scene of Bill's past about a decade ago when he was still in the nursing home."

"There are three people around him. They're speaking to him. No, instructing him. Bill appears to be very upset. He's making sounds, but he's not speaking. I can hear the others—" Karen says.

"Bessie, you distract him; I'll get his shirt on," commands the smallest but eldest nurse, Nurse Gretchen.

"Distract him, heck! Last time I got near him, he bit me. I was off three days from work. Nurse Brenda can engage him, and if he gets a hold of her, I'll hit him," responds Bessie, the biggest of the three nurses.

"You'll do no such thing," responds Gretchen. Now, turning toward Brenda, the youngest nurse, apparently a trainee, she says, "You just watch this, honey." Turning toward Bill, the nurse starts to sing, "Take me out to the ball game, take me out to the park …" which starts to calm Bill down. Bill begins to sing. He knows the rhythm and words, but the words don't come, only basic unintelligible syllables in a rough approximation of the melody.

"Tad, tat a tat a baaa baaa…" sings Bill as he gestures his head.

"Wow. I didn't know he could sing. I thought his brain dam—" Brenda says as she's interrupted.

"Nurse Brenda, hush! Come over here. Bill's brain is severely damaged, but he still has considerable mental capacity. Enough to know what he's lost. He understands everything we say and do. He's lost control of his motor functions and speech, but his intellectual capacity hasn't been totally diminished. His is a strong mind held prisoner in a broken body, so don't talk down to him or talk about him in his presence."

"I'm sorry, Nurse Gretchen. I didn't know," says Brenda.

"I know, Nurse Brenda. Just remember, being a nurse means caring for people. I've seen nurses hurt Bill so bad he cried for hours, just in saying careless things," Gretchen says.

"I'll be more careful. Thanks," Brenda says.

"Bill was a baseball player in college," Gretchen says.

"He went to college?" asked Brenda.

"Yes, Bill went to college. He was a doctor. Bill's background information is buried in the archived section of his chart; I put his original chart together about five years ago when he was admitted," Gretchen says. She continues, "Bill had a beautiful wife and two wonderful kids. And then came the car accident that put him here. A school bus driver had a heart attack one day driving an empty bus—he had just dropped the kids off at school. His bus careened into Bill's lane, and without even thinking (according to the police, Bill didn't have time to think), he drove his car off the road and into an oncoming truck to avoid hitting a school bus full of children. The accident left him with multiple severe brain contusions, subdural hematoma, edema, and a broken neck at C6 and C7. His family came for a short time to visit him. But as soon as they realized he wasn't going to get any better, they stopped visiting. First, the wife stopped coming; she just dropped off the kids. Then the kids stopped. There was no way for them to communicate or do anything. Can't really blame them, I suppose. He has original family, but they're out of town, and they haven't been here for a couple of years. Not a soul ever comes to visit Bill anymore."

"I'm so sorry to hear all this," responds Brenda through tears. "I'll learn that baseball song and sing it to him every chance I get."

"Now that's the quality of a real nurse. I'll teach it to you…" Gretchen says.

A few moments later, AJ's face comes back into Karen's view.

"Wow, AJ. I don't know if I'm more overwhelmed by what I just witnessed or by what I just experienced. It was like I was really there eavesdropping on someone else's life. I feel real empathy for Bill as if he were my wounded brother," Karen says.

"Bill is your wounded brother, and you'll meet him soon. He plays all positions, and his favorite position is the one he's playing at that moment (AJ laughs). It doesn't matter which position it is; he just loves the game. At this particular time, I understand he's playing shortstop for the Radical Ruths. And Bill's wound is almost healed. Soon, he'll be ready to mentor his first buddy."

AJ says he has business on Earth, blesses the ladies, and returns to Earth.

Chapter 22

Bert has been seeing Margareta for about four weeks now, and stress from her demands, mounting bills, and sustained alcohol consumption is taking a toll. When Bert arrives home this evening, he finds Roy comfortably settled in his chair, engrossed in the television program. Bert immediately explodes and throws the bills at Roy as he moves toward him. "What the heck are you do'n in my chair and watching my TV?" yells Bert as he grabs Roy and throws him to the floor.

"I'm sorry, Dad. I didn't mean—"

"You good for nothing, brat—" As Bert raises his hand to slap Roy, he knocks over the remote from the arm of the chair to the floor. The remote opens up, and batteries roll on the floor. "Look what you did, you son-of-a—you broke my TV!"

"I'm sorry, Dad. I didn't mean to—" But instead of escalating the abuse, Bert redirects his attention to the remote and the batteries.

"Get to your room, boy. I'll deal with you later!"

Roy goes to bed that night without supper. But he also goes to bed none the worse for wear. It is almost like an angel knocked over the remote to distract Bert. Whatever it was, it worked, at least for this night.

"When there's no food, we find that real sustenance is found in God," AJ says. "I'll quote you some Psalms, Roy, as you fall to sleep." AJ quotes several Psalms to Roy, beginning with the 23rd. Roy cannot hear the words but receives a blessing nonetheless and falls peacefully to sleep.

AJ observes Bert and Margarita planning their civil wedding and honeymoon in Vegas. Bert's parents will stay with Roy for their long weekend away. AJ watches as one demon is now speaking to both Bert and Margareta (apparently, Margareta's demon has been reassigned). The demon appears solid and substantial and is speaking with a loud voice that sounds to AJ like a dog incessantly barking. Neither AJ nor the demon acknowledges each other's presence; it seems that the jurisdiction of each kingdom is a sovereign domain. The demon now has a name, Poison.

AJ tries to speak wisdom to Bert and Margareta: "It's so fast. You should get to know more about each other. Bert, you should focus on Melody and—" when Poison rebukes AJ, "They're both mine! You have no power here. Leave them alone!"

Bert and Margareta, during the engagement stage, spend about half of their time overnighting at Margareta's apartment, leaving Roy alone at night and seldom with any notice. When they stay at Bert's, their conjugal relations (and arguments) disturb Roy so much that he plays the radio all night. No investment in Roy or Melody's absence is characteristic of their time and attention.

AJ turns his attention to Melody (Crescenda). The young (unmarried) couple's first few days are kind of a poor man's honeymoon. Neither Derek nor Melody are worried about the future or the present, except Derek reminds Melody she needs to find a job. Melody continues to go to school but skips many of her classes. She starts looking for a part-time job and lands one at a neighborhood convenience store. She works evenings, mostly stocking and doing inventory. After several weeks, Melody musters the courage to tell Derek she is pregnant.

It's been about four weeks since she discovered she was pregnant, and the morning sickness has just about stopped. Melody spends countless hours discussing how to tell Derek with her friends. She attends almost no classes and does no classwork or homework. Her friends come up with a short list of ideas. Melody decides on a sweet and positive approach and uses the money she earned in her first job to show Derek that neither she nor their baby will burden Derek.

When Derek comes home from work the evening of Melody's day off, Melody makes a nice dinner and serves him. Derek is impressed. "That was a good dinner. Thanks, Melody. What's the special occasion?"

Melody, with trembling hands, gives Derek a wrapped package.

"Wow! A gift for me? Thanks," Derek exclaims, and starts to open the package. "What are these? Baby shoes? I don't get it; what do I want with baby shoes?"

"We're going to have a baby, Derek. We're going to have a family," Melody says.

"A baby! What the heck? I don't want a darn baby!" Derek responds.

Melody starts to cry. "I'm sorry," she says.

"Wait, don't cry. Maybe we can work this out somehow," Derek says. "I don't know, I'll have to give this some thought." Which Melody takes to mean, *OK, I'm over the shock and adjusting to the idea of a baby, becoming a father, and being a husband.*

Derek thinks that perhaps they could extort some investment from Melody's father. "Do you think your dad would help us out? You know, invest in us and the baby. Maybe we could name it after him if it's a boy," Derek says. Melody discourages the concept, telling Derek her dad's not interested in her, anyone, or anything besides himself. So, Derek begins to sour more and more on the relationship.

***

Over the next several days, as Melody starts to talk about her dream of future life (marriage, finances, the baby), Derek goes non-linear.

He has no intention of marrying her or being a father—it's her baby, nothing else. "You decide. You're outta here!" Derek proclaims.

Derek tells Melody to leave; she can go back home or wherever, but get out tonight. Melody cries and argues she has nowhere to go, but she'll leave tomorrow. Derek aggressively storms out of the apartment and heads to a friend's, telling Melody she better be gone when he returns tomorrow. "Just get you and your baby out of my apartment!" Derek demands.

Melody has no idea what she's gonna do, so she starts phoning and texting as soon as her hysteria subsides a bit. None of her friends were able to help, except one of her friends offered to ask her parents if she could stay there for a while until she got on her feet. Then Melody remembered a young woman at work named Linda, who had an apartment and was complaining about the expense. Maybe she needed a roommate? So, she packed up her things and stored them secretly at the home of another one of her girlfriends, just temporarily until she found a place. She went to work later that day to ask Linda if she wanted a roommate. She did, and the two agreed that Melody could move in with her.

"I just broke up with my boyfriend, Derek; he's such a jerk. He said he loved me, but he only wanted sex—"

"Girl. Don't you know it? That's all any of them want—"

AJ returns to Paradise.

Chapter 23

As the ladies' conversation concludes, they arrive at Fenway Park. The stadium appears to seat about fifty thousand fans. There are no commercial billboards, only billboards of Scripture verses and praise to the Lord. The announcers have an incredible sound system so that fans can hear each word perfectly. And there's a taste of the Minor League, such as the organ, and various fun sound effects, like a windshield being broken by a foul ball. There are many seats around the field, and the fans have about half the seats filled. Fans constantly come and go. AJ and Nora escort Karen to the bullpen. They ask one of the players who the manager is, and he points to a teen who looks to be about fourteen years of age and says: "Kirby Puckett, right over there, he's our manager."

"Hello, Kirby. I'm Angel Jaynes. Just call me AJ. I want to introduce Nora and Karen to you. Karen's a big baseball fan and would like to join the Radical Ruths."

"Hello, AJ, Nora, Karen, I'm Kirby. I'm glad to meet you. And welcome to the Radical Ruths, Karen. What position do you play?"

"I'm so thrilled to meet you, Mr. Puckett. I've read so much about you. I remember you in the '87 World Series! I just can't believe it's really you."

"Didn't think I'd make it? That's okay, neither did I. But God's grace is greater than my issues," Kirby says.

"Oh, no, sir. I'm sor—"

"Nonsense, I was just yanking your chain, Karen; lighten up, this is a fun place. Now, what position do you play?"

"I don't know. None, really. I mean, I played shortstop in softball mostly and second base a few times."

"That's fine, Karen. We'll start you out at shortstop. We're playing the Yeshua's Yankees; it's all tied up—it always is, we don't keep score. God doesn't keep score."

"Kirby, does the name Yeshua's Yankees imply that the Lord's favorite team is the Yankees?" Nora asks.

"No, the Lord has no favorites." After a brief dramatic pause, Kirby leans in toward Karen and says: "But there has been speculation that the Lord has always had a soft spot for His Yankees." The group laughs, and Kirby motions to a young man and calls him over. "This is my defensive coach, Lou. Lou, meet Karen. She's your new shortstop."

"Hello, Karen, welcome to the Radical Ruths. We're glad to have ya, Shorty. Come on, I'll introduce you to the rest of the team."

"Is that who I think it is?" whispers Nora to Kirby.

"The Iron Horse himself, Lou Gehrig," Kirby replies.

"Wow, incredible. I heard so much about him on the radio, listening to games with my dad. It's such a small universe."

"Miss Nora, you wouldn't believe the players in our league and some in the other leagues here in Paradise. But the real story is the average player, like Karen. They don't have the name recognition among people as the Babe, Sandy, Jolt'n Joe, or the hundreds of other big names we have heard in Paradise, but they're as well known, loved, and important to God as any celebrity, sports or otherwise. God is so gracious!" says Kirby.

"Amen," AJ and Nora say in unison, along with everyone else who heard the comment.

E. Vince

Nora and AJ sit in the stands next to a mature man and an older-looking child. They're discussing the game. AJ waits for a polite pause in the conversation and then asks, "What inning is it?"

"The best I can tell is it's about the 3,917th inning. If you don't count the roughly 560 innings they played against the Obadiah Orioles before they restructured," responds the elderly gentleman.

Nora inquires of AJ, "Since the teams don't keep score, why do we care about the inning?"

"We don't, really. It's just that the convention is the home team's at bat during the even innings. I really just wanted to know whether it was even or odd," AJ responds.

"Who's at bat now? I don't recognize him," asks AJ.

"That's Henry Neumann; he's a good kid, looks to be about eight years old, I'd say. He was a plumber from Cincinnati. He's been in Paradise for a while but just recently started playing ball."

"Well, if I'm not mistaken, I counted about seven strikes on Henry so far."

"Actually, I believe it's more like seventeen. He was at bat before you sat down. But that's okay; he'll hit it eventually. Ah, there's a hit! Way to go, Henry!" The crowd goes wild as Henry runs to first.

"Where are my manners? I'm William, and this is my buddy, Frank," says the elderly gentleman.

"And this is Nora, and I am Angel Jaynes. We're pleased to meet you, gents."

"Do you have someone special on one of the two teams?" asks Frank.

"Yes, Karen, the brand-new shortstop for the Ruths," responds Nora.

"There seems to be something special about her. She appears happy, but she's sad, or perhaps distressed," says Frank.

"That's curious; she's quite happy, but thanks for your concern, Frank," responds Nora.

"Since you two are hitting it off so well, I bid you adieu for now," says AJ.

"Wait, AJ. What's Frank concerned about? Is there some sort of problem with Karen?" Nora asks.

"I really don't know. I've not been made aware of a problem, at least not yet. But let's keep our eyes open," AJ says.

AJ returns to Earth.

Chapter 24

AJ returns to observe how Melody is getting on. On one of the few days Melody goes to school, she walks by the counselor's office and thinks, *I need some adult advice*. She stops at the office and decides to wait for an opening.

After hearing Melody's story, Ms. Stint, the school counselor, launches into assertive counselor mode. "Melody, you're in much pain right now, and you're feeling alone and desperate. But you're not alone, and I'm here to help you. You have your whole life in front of you, and there's no reason that a little mistake should ruin your whole life. I want you to see this doctor. Here's his card. He can help you. We're not going to let this thing destroy your whole life. Make an appointment. If my schedule permits, I'll drive you there; if not, I'll find you a ride," says Ms. Stint.

"Do you mean an abortion? I don't think I can do that," says Melody.

"Yes, Melody, I mean an abortion. Do you want this child? How are you going to take care of it? You said the father abandoned you. You're just a few weeks along, and it's not a baby; it's just a mass of tissue. And you can't let a mass of tissue destroy your life. It's the same with any mass of tissue, like cancer. If you get cancer or a tumor, you cut it out to save your life. It's the same thing here; it is just a mass of tissue, and you need to cut it out. And I'm going to help you make that decision. Someday, you'll thank me."

"I'm so scared, I don't know what to do," Melody says, hands and body trembling, then breaks into a full cry.

"I know. I'm here to help you."

After a brief moment she asks, "Don't I have to tell my dad? What will he say?"

"No. This is your body. This is your life. And nobody has the right to interfere. I will call the clinic and accompany you to the appointment; this is too important. I'll rearrange my calendar as necessary. You're not alone, Melody, and once this is done, the prospects for your life will seem wonderful again. I promise," says the counselor.

So, Ms. Stint makes the arrangements, hugs Melody, and sends her off to go home on an excused absence. But Melody heads to the third-floor girl's bathroom, where she hopes her friends will be hanging out smoking cigarettes and weed. One of her not-too-close friends is in the girls' bathroom, and Melody shares her dilemma and decision. The friend is shocked and tries to talk her out of the abortion, but Melody has no hope. Derek abandoned her, so she's done with this mass of tissue. Perhaps, she feels, she can at least hurt Derek indirectly this way.

***

About a week later, Ms. Stint escorts Melody to the appointment at the local clinic. The clinic counselor informs Melody, through tears and near hysteria, that she really does want an abortion and to get this all quickly behind her. Melody is hijacked into the abortion; she doesn't know she has any other options. She's given the prescription, a couple of instructions, and some written material—much too complex for someone of her age and in her state. The counselor drives her to within a block of her home, and she walks the rest of the way home armed with the weapon that is about to take her little mistake's life.

For the first time in all eternity, past and present, AJ tears up.

AJ returns to Paradise.

Chapter 25

Karen plays for the Radical Ruths for the equivalent of about three Earth months. Karen meets Bill, who mentors her in infield best practices. She learns and plays in several positions. Karen develops spiritually from about eleven to sixteen years old; she's now a young woman. Near the end of Karen's first term with the team, the Radical Ruths are scheduled for a series of away games. The first is at Comiskey Park to play a series with the Lord's Sox. Then they head to Dodger Stadium to play a series against Daniel's Dodgers. Karen (on Earth) always loved the Dodgers and can't resist transferring to that team, where she plays second base for about one Earth month. In all, she plays ball for the equivalent of roughly six Earth months. As a young woman, Karen's beginning to ask about her purpose, mission, and service to the Lord and the others in Paradise. *Besides, I'm already the best infielder the game's ever seen,* Karen thinks to herself. *Time to master something else.*

After consultation with Nora, Karen decides to visit some historical persons while exploring Paradise. "If there's one thing I like almost as much as baseball, it's history," Karen remarks to Nora.

The ladies begin their adventure by walking through Belush'ya and then proceeding on to Servern'ya, by way of the Library. AJ explains that Belush'ya is the entry portal to Paradise for all human souls destined for Heaven, and its angel is the Archangel Zadkiel (the Ecology Angel, responsible for stewardship of Earth's ecosystems). AJ further explains that Karen can't see Zadkiel yet since he's an

Archangel and stands directly in the presence of God, but someday, she'll be able to see archangels.

"You're my Archangel, AJ," Karen says.

"Thank you, Daughter," AJ responds, "but you can't possibly understand. It's not your fault, but you will someday see and experience holiness, goodness, love, and light that are more awesome than the sun or even UY Scuti. That's what being in the presence of an Archangel is like. And archangels hide their faces before the awesome God."

"So, clearly, no person is able to stand in God's presence on their own merit," Nora says. "It seems like we need God's grace just to abide in His presence. God must be far beyond human comprehension."

"That, my sister, is the understatement of eternity," AJ responds.

"What will we encounter on our journey?" Karen asks.

"Servern'ya is the city of the Archangel Chamuel, and it's the city of servants, which includes martyrs," AJ explains. Karen recalls that her spiritual mission is servanthood. "You will encounter beauty and peace, brothers and sisters, angels, hospitality, love, and adventure," AJ answers.

Purity Path is the road from Belush'ya, where the trio is currently located, to the Library. It's explained that each person has at least one mission from God, which is related to their spiritual gift; servanthood is one of those missions, and all children of God with the mission of servanthood live primarily in Servern'ya while learning the mission and acquiring advanced skills (though all are free to travel and reside ad lib.).

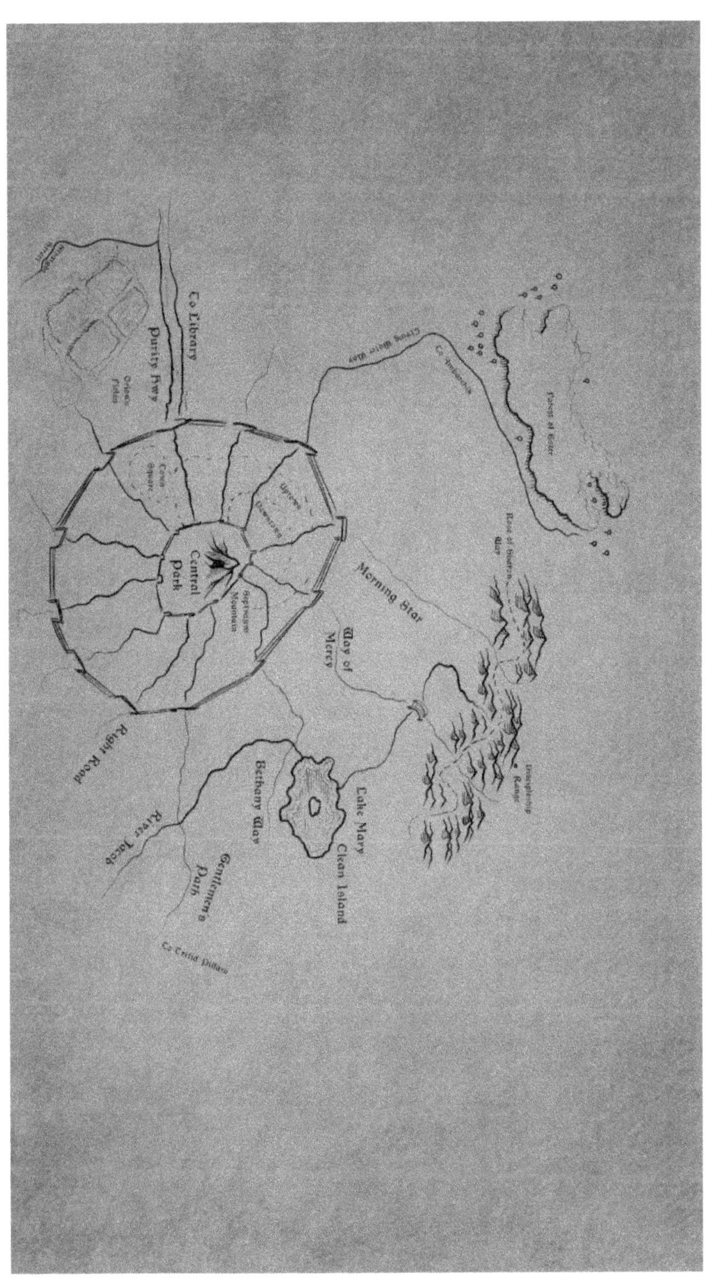

Figure 2 The Belush'ya School for Young Souls

AJ says, "There are many, but they can be classified at a high level; according to this scroll." AJ then hands it to the ladies.

- Servanthood, personified by the Archangel Chamuel and centered in the city of Servern'ya; the uniform of Archangel Chamuel, all his angels, and all the people with the mission of servanthood is a yellow toga over a white tunic and a white belt.

- Leadership, personified by the Archangel Gabriel and centered in the city of Antares; the uniform of Archangel Gabriel, all his angels, and all the people with the mission of leadership is a blue toga over a white tunic and a gold sash.

- Healing, personified by the Archangel Azrael and centered in the city of Nova'ya; the uniform of Archangel Azrael, all his angels, and all the people with the mission of healing, is a white toga over a white tunic and a silver sash.

- Martial Arts (i.e., the host or army of heaven), personified by the Archangel Michael and centered in the city of Ambarchik; the uniform of Archangel Michael, all his angels, and all the people with the mission of martial arts is a red toga over a white tunic and a silver sash.

- Worship, personified by the Archangel Uriel and centered in the city of Trifid Pillars; the uniform of Archangel Uriel, all his angels, and all the people with the mission of worship is a purple toga over a white tunic and a gold sash.

- Intercession, personified by the Archangel Raphael and centered in the city of Lapteva; the uniform of Archangel Raphael, all his angels, and all the people with the mission of intercession is an orange toga over a white tunic and a green sash.

- Resources, Hospitality, and Ecology personified by the Archangel Zadkiel and centered in the city of Belush'ya; the uniform of Archangel Zadkiel, all his angels, and all the people with the mission of resources, hospitality, and ecology is a green toga over a white tunic and an orange belt.

AJ explains to Karen that there's no hierarchy implied in the missions or colors; each mission is necessary and sufficient for God's purposes and complements her decision to explore the Havens (a local name for Paradise) beginning at Servern'ya to speak with and learn from other servants.

Karen's company walks out of Belush'ya from one of the West Gates (specifically John's Gate) toward the Library. They see many people entering and leaving the city. All entering are welcomed into the city by a Welcoming Committee just outside the gate, and all exiting the city are blessed by a Blessing Committee just inside the gate.

The Welcoming and Blessing Committee's membership is dynamic; people join and leave the committees ad lib. Some visitors just stand around in awe of the beauty as they enter the city. Others are kneeling in prayer or thanksgiving. And many worship by kneeling, standing, singing, and some by dancing.

Most of the Blessing Committee wear green togas with orange belts, but there's a mix, indicating that some of the Belush'ya Blessing Team members are from other cities. Several people kiss Nora and Karen on the cheek and look them straight and deep into their eyes when they pronounce their blessings.

"I hate to leave this beautiful city, but every city, town, or village must be equally pleasant," Karen says. "What did you like best about it, Nora? I loved the tree-lined boulevards, Central Park, and the art deco in the Greenwich section of the city; even though I was quite young, I can always appreciate art," Karen continues.

"I loved the endless variety of wildflowers and the absolute cleanliness of everything, everywhere. But each place we visit and all the roadways between places will be just as beautiful," Nora replies.

It's becoming just a bit more difficult for Karen to distinguish between angels and human beings. The more spiritually mature folks are beginning to look a bit more like angels, she notes in amusement—she doesn't know whether it's because she's maturing and seeing things differently now or whether people or angels are actually changing.

"Nora, AJ said that God gives every person a gift and a mission. What's yours?" asks Karen.

"My gifts are ministry and exhortation. My mission is servanthood. Do you know your gifts yet?"

"No, just my mission, servanthood, but yours are very cool. I can see these gifts in you. I'm so honored to have you as my buddy," remarks Karen with a few tears of joy.

"I just bet God's given you several gifts, Karen. Let's ask AJ; he'll know," suggests Nora.

Just up the road ahead, they see AJ walking toward them, and they exchange greetings. "So, Karen, you want to know your spiritual gifts?" asks AJ.

"Yes, please, if it's permitted for me to know them now."

"Of course it is. Your gifts are compassion and giving."

As AJ speaks these words, the Holy Spirit quickens these gifts in Karen, and she gasps: "Oh my!" Karen, followed by Nora and AJ, then fall to their knees and begin thanking and praising God. Still overwhelmed with joy, Karen slowly rises to her feet, AJ helping both Karen and Nora a bit.

"I just can't believe how good God is. He's restored my life and health, He's made me one of His children, He's given me gifts and a purpose. I'm just so overwhelmed to experience God's love for me."

"Amen," declare Nora and AJ in unison.

AJ returns to Earth.

Chapter 26

"Greetings, AJ. It's been a while since I've had the pleasure of your company. To what do I owe the gift of your presence here on Earth?" asks Angel Sarai.

"Thanks, Sarai, you're so encouraging. Likewise, I've longed for your company as well. I'm heading back to my Karen's Melody. She's struggling terribly, about to commit abortion," AJ says.

"Your Karen? My, you seem to have developed some uncharacteristic attachment to these wild beasts," Sarai says.

"No, not really. I know how the Almighty suffers at the plight of these creatures. As far as I'm concerned, I can take 'em or leave 'em," AJ replies.

"Ah, thanks for clarifying, AJ. It's no sin to change your mind when you realize that just perhaps your previous judgments may have been premature and/or harsh."

"If and when I come to that realization, I certainly will repent, Sarai, and you'll be the second to know," AJ responds.

"I am sorry to hear that your Melody is suffering. You know, of course, that it's likely to get much darker before the dawn?" asks Sarai. "Do you know the name of the baby yet?"

"His name is Fred," responds AJ. "He'll be welcomed here among the half a billion aborted and killed babies very soon now."

"Yes, I know," Sarai replies.

"Please remember us in your prayers. Until next time—our Lord's continued blessing of His mission and ministry through you," are the parting words of AJ to AS.

AJ arrives at Linda's apartment just as Melody's taking the RU-486. Crescenda (Melody) becomes very sick; she thinks it was seeing the fetus in the toilet, but the sickness doesn't go away after several days; rather, it intensifies. She returns to the clinic, and they tell her to go to the ER. The ER doc says she has septicemia (the doc doesn't tell her that it was from a rotting part of her dead baby still in the uterus, which didn't abort). She was gravely ill for several weeks, so she was fired from the convenience store. The antibiotic regime she was on had its own set of side effects, which Crescenda poorly managed.

Crescenda eventually recovers while bumming at Linda's apartment. She gets a new job and begins to share Linda's expenses. After a couple of months, Crescenda develops a love of parties. Crescenda is too preoccupied with partying to invest any effort into work, so after about forty days on the job, Crescenda is fired. At first, Linda tries to give Crescenda a hand up and extend patience. But after several months of listening to excuses, Linda evicts Crescenda.

"I liked you better when you were Melody," Linda comments. A silhouette speaks to Crescenda, "I like me. Finally, I'm myself; ain't nobody gonna mess with me…"

AJ tries, to no avail, to speak light and truth to Crescenda. The demon just laughs and taunts AJ as Crescenda's abject rejection of truth and light progresses. "She's mine!" growls the demon.

"Melody was a rug everybody walked on. Crescenda's a fighter no one will ever take advantage of. I like Crescenda," Crescenda retorts.

"I'm glad you like Crescenda because I don't, and I'm tired of covering your expenses and you bringing home drunken men at all hours. I want you to leave," Linda says.

"After all the help I've been to you, you dus gonna kick me out? What the heck is dis? You one nasty tramp, hussy. I'm outta here, and don't be comin' 'round looking for me to bail your sorry arse out!" Crescenda yells.

Crescenda's on the phone, in her bedroom, looking for someone to take her in; she promises her female acquaintances she'll pay rent and help with expenses, even though she's unemployed, and she promises her male acquaintances an express trip to the moon (every day). She gets no takers, so she'll have to resume her house hunting tomorrow.

AJ looks in on Bert before returning to Paradise. Bert and Margareta got married in Vegas per plan. Roy enjoyed his grandparents' stay at the house. It was one of the few times he could recall predictability, orderliness, and nurturing in his present reality. He wished they never had to leave, or better yet, that he "could go with them."

The honeymoon's over, and the newlyweds have already developed significant problems. Margareta was also previously married, and her first husband, Pancho, was consistently unfaithful, so she was very untrusting and suspicious. "I'm going out with some friends for a few drinks," Bert says.

"Going out? What friends?" Poison says to Margareta.

"What do you mean going out? For how long? Where? And what friends?" Margareta asks accusingly.

"What's all this baloney?" Poison says to Bert. "I'm going out for a few drinks. What's your problem?"

"What's all this twenty-questions blarney?" Bert responds. "I said I'm just going out to have a few drinks with my friends. What's your problem with that?"

"He's going to see another woman. No doubt about it. He's cheating on me already!" Poison says to Margareta.

"You're going to see a woman, aren't you?" Margareta yells.

"If you don't stop ragging on me, I will be seeing another woman!" Bert yells as he exits the house, slamming the door behind him. Poison laughs long and hearty, very pleased with himself.

Bert never processed the grief of losing Karen. He just stifled the emotions, so he's always comparing Margareta and Karen and is always unhappy. Bert forgets he was also unhappy with Karen.

AJ returns to Paradise.

Chapter 27

The trio continues on their journey toward the Library. After what seems to be just a short time, they begin to not just hear but feel the most exquisite music coming from in the distance up ahead. Karen enters into a reflective meditation in sync with the music. Nora feels like a slow waltz driving her thoughts and actions. AJ has a peaceful smile on his face. This section of Purity Path is a wide gravel road meandering through an expansive country meadow with scattered trees and oceans of wildflowers. "We're going to experience an amazing encounter after this next bend in the road," AJ says to the ladies.

It's an orchestra of immense size in an enormous pavilion just off the road. It would seem to have at least a thousand instrumentalists and a choir of approximately three times that size. The musicians consist of both people and angels. There seem to be hundreds of people and angels who are not part of the choir or orchestra as talent but are supervisors or leaders of some sort, coaching and mentoring the talent. There appear to be scores of angels and people coordinating between the section leaders and senior leadership. Then there are tens of liaisons between the coordinators and a few leaders of the orchestra and choir; these few then report to a single assistant conductor of the orchestra and one of the choir. Finally, there is one conductor, an elder, the maestro, who appears both stern and compassionate at the same time. Wild hair, passionate moves, emoting and evoking an almost frightening level of passion in the choir and orchestra might be terrifying if the music weren't so beautiful. This elder conductor is obviously a person of immense stature in Paradise; the entire ensemble follows his every instruction to the utmost detail. The music is rapturous, the most beautiful thing either of the ladies has yet to experience in Paradise thus far.

"This is the most beautiful thing I've ever experienced, but I don't comprehend it," Nora says.

"Who could comprehend such a thing, Nora? It's like living music. I don't understand it either," responds Karen.

"Only God could fully comprehend a thing of such beauty," Nora replies.

"Did you know that God loves music?" asks AJ.

"No, but now that you say it, it seems perfectly right," answers Nora.

"This choir and orchestra are working on a specially commissioned piece," AJ continues.

"Really? What?" asks Nora.

"Why don't you ask the maestro?" AJ responds.

"Oh, I couldn't. He's so busy, and the whole ensemble is hanging on his every gesture," replies Nora.

"It's alright, I assure you. Come meet Beethoven."

"Beethoven!"

"Yes, come."

The three head down to the pavilion where Beethoven stands conducting. They sit in the stands just in back of the maestro and listen in a state of rapture. Eventually, one of the liaisons notices the three, approaches them, and asks if he could be of any service. AJ explains, "We are the company of Karen, Nora, and Angel Jaynes, and they'd like to speak briefly with Beethoven." The liaison, who goes by the name of Vivaldi, indicates it would be no problem. Vivaldi motions to Beethoven and gets his attention, then points to the three behind him.

Beethoven turns around briefly and then quickly returns to the orchestra and gives them a soft landing. He then walks over toward the three.

"Welcome, good folks. How may this humble servant of the Lord help you?"

"I am Angel Jaynes. These are Nora and Karen. They heard your music while passing by and wanted to meet you and ask you about your special commission."

"Wonderful, but it's not my music. I have the privilege of composing and conducting, but it's all of our music and the Lord's music. I've been given the greatest honor God has ever given any person or angel. God has commissioned me (brief pause while Beethoven regains his composure), me to write and conduct the music for (another brief interlude for Beethoven to get the following words out)—the Marriage Supper of the Lamb."

"Hollowed be Thy Name," is then said by all present in a most solemn and sacred manner.

"What's the Marriage Supper of the Lamb?" Karen asks.

"No one knows for sure, but I believe its significance is that it's the final act of the Lord's salvation. That is, humankind has been justified, sanctified, and glorified, and this marriage step is the fulfillment of the New Covenant, where God and humankind become One," AJ responds.

Beethoven comments, "I can't believe the goodness of God. His mercy and His loving kindness (another brief moment of silence while the maestro again composes himself) are of such surpassing magnitude that even my great sin is atoned for. I was so unbelieving and unfaithful to God, angry at God while I was alive. Now, I'm awestruck by God's goodness to me and His long-suffering with me. Had the Lord allowed me to enter Paradise as the apprentice street sweeper, it would have been better than I deserved. Yet the Lord gave me this mission despite my imperfections and failures. 'Thank You, my Heavenly Father, for Your loving kindness and tender mercies, but mostly for Your salvation through your Son, my Lord and Savior. Amen. Ich Habe Genug.'"

"Amen," is again said solemnly by all present.

"The Lord permitted me to work with this remarkable talent you see before you—Vivaldi, Bach, Mendelssohn, and Elvis, to name a few. We collaborate on orchestral and chorale pieces. Each choir and orchestra member is of consummate skill and dedication. The angelic members have unbelievable musical gifts, the likes of which still have me in awe," Beethoven says.

"I'm sorry, but I still don't understand. What is the Marriage Supper of the Lamb? What does this mean?" Karen asks again.

"No one knows for sure—neither man nor angel, but only God. However, we do know that Israel and the church are joined into one and will become the Lord's Bride and that there will be a wedding ceremony, and somehow, in some mysterious way, God and man will be joined. I don't understand it, but that is the theme of my composition. It just pours out from me without ceasing," Beethoven says.

"God and man will be joined?" remarks Karen in almost a whisper of utter solemnitude.

"Yes. And it's not so unbelievable, really. Remember, man was made in God's own image and for the purpose of an unending relationship with God. Someday soon, the collective of redeemed mankind will be transformed into the pure, holy, and incorruptible beauty the Lord originally intended; the Lord's Bride and God will be eternally joined," AJ remarks.

"Even more so than now? I feel so close to God. His love is almost palpable," says Nora.

"Even more than now. And there is another secret aspect even more wonderful, but we shall not speak of it now," admonishes AJ.

"Thank you for taking time for us, maestro. May the Lord continue to bless His mission and ministry through you and your passion," AJ says.

"Thank you, my friends, and may the Lord likewise continue to shine His love and mercies upon you lavishly," Beethoven responds.

The troop takes their leave of Beethoven, and the maestro calls the ensemble back to readiness and then begins again to conduct. The three are played along their path for what seems like many miles with hauntingly beautiful music.

"Beethoven's been working on this commission for about two hundred Earth years," AJ remarks as they return to their journey.

"Two hundred years, unbelievable. But I guess a work of such monumental scope and beauty takes a long time," Nora remarks.

"Yes, but it's almost finished. All of Heaven is waiting in anxious anticipation for the debut of this work, the wedding ceremony, the Bride to be made perfect and holy, and the Groom's appearance. It will be the happiest time Heaven has ever experienced," says AJ.

"Amen," is said in unison by the company.

AJ takes his leave as the ladies continue toward the Library.

Chapter 28

"I declare, Nora, that AJ sure comes and goes."

"Yes, he does, and it's such a comfort knowing he's always ready to coach in any way needed," Nora says. "It appears to me that you've aged spiritually. I'd guess you're maybe seventeen or eighteen."

"Really? I think I feel it, too," Karen responds. "Strange, I just realized something for the first time. Even though he's an angel, AJ doesn't seem to evoke the male attractiveness I remember when I walked the Earth. In fact, none of the human males here in Paradise do either," Karen comments.

"That's right. And the males' feelings toward us seem to be mutual. They don't appear to find us attractive in the female way. It's such a wonderful comfort to be able to have relationships without any sexual tension," Nora says.

"Amen," says Karen. Then she asks, "Since there doesn't seem to be any sexual tension in Paradise, how do married couples here relate to each other?"

"Just like everyone else relates, we're now all sisters and brothers. People who were married are no longer married. We're all just family here," says Nora.

"That's so beautiful. And non-threatening," Karen remarks. After a brief moment of thought, Karen asks, "So everyone in Paradise is sexually pure?"

"Not just sexually pure but pure in every sense. Pure in love, in faith, in serving God and others, and we all practice integrity in all relationships," Nora replies.

"Wow! I'd say this is Heaven on Earth, but we're not on Earth, are we?" asks Karen.

"No. Paradise is not on Earth, but I'm not sure where it is. I just know it is, and God is, and we are," Nora says again.

"If all people here in Paradise are practicing purity, even the young ones, then as we become spiritually more mature, are we practicing purity better or more completely?" Karen asks.

"I don't think so, Karen. I believe purity is the absence of corruption. So, to be in a state of purity means that we are all equally free from corruption, regardless of our spiritual maturity. This is God's gift to us. I believe our spiritual maturity reflects our closeness to God, how much we love God, and how much we resemble God—in terms of His image growing in us," Nora responds.

"I see. Then it's probably accurate to say that purity is a given for all in Paradise, people and angels," Karen says.

"Yes, I believe that's correct. It's a gift. God somehow grants us the purity of His Son as he transforms us into the image of His Son. Don't ask me to explain how, sister. I don't know how, but I see the evidence all around me: the loving kindness of everyone we meet, the welcoming and unconditional acceptance we also receive, and the goodness in everyone's eyes," Nora says.

A while later, as the ladies walk in silence for the first time in a while, they see a group approaching them. There is a man who seems to be the center of attention of the group, comprised of a few persons and several angels. The man appears middle-aged and is wearing a laurel wreath and a dazzling white robe with a bright red sash. "The man wearing the crown and sash is a martyr. He died rather than deny the Lord. He, and all martyrs, receive special recognition and honor in Paradise among both men and angels," explains Nora as they approach greeting distance.

"Blessed be the Name of the Lord. I'm Nora and this is Karen, humble servants of God and our fellow men," announces Nora.

"May the Lord reign in you and magnify His glory through you. We are in the company of Philip, the martyr, highly favored by God. We bid you peace," responds a spokesman for the company.

"Will you tarry a moment with us, honored elders?" asks Nora.

"We will, fellow children of our God," answers the spokesman.

The long grass of the meadow mixed with opulent flowers quilts to form a self-assembled bank of cushions just off the side of the road as the group prepared to establish a venue. The group steps onto the quilted grass and flower mixture and spreads out sheets for the people to sit on. They prepare a lovely banquet of fruits, bread, and wine. Philip the martyr offers thanksgiving to God, and the group enjoys a light repast and conversation. Birds fly above, short and long-stemmed flowers sway gently in the soft breeze, and clouds meander slowly above the horizon. The ambient temperature and humidity are most comfortable and pleasing.

During the conversation, Karen leans in a bit toward Philip and politely asks, "You are a martyr. May I ask what happened? Is that permitted?"

"Yes, sister, it is permitted. I was an orphaned child in the village of Heglig in southern Sudan. Muslim raiders killed my father; my mother was brutally hurt and left for dead. These were the same men who had ravished my village several times before. Each time they would kill the men, and if they could find the women, they would rape and attack them, too. They would offer to give food to anyone who would deny Jesus and convert to Islam. A few women and children usually relented and were allowed to live, and many refused and were killed. Sometimes, the martyrs were shot, but usually, they were hacked to death or beaten to death, or sometimes burned to death—bullets eventually became too precious to expend on us. My mother was still alive for a while after they hurt her. But she became very sick and then delirious with a high fever. She died several days after the attack; she was in such pain, and I had no medicine or comfort for her. So, I did the only thing I could do: I sang to her, and she tried to smile when I sang. I made a shelter of some branches over her to keep her out of the direct sunlight. She was too heavy for me to move back to the village to a shelter. I buried her as deep as I could, right where she died, to keep the jackals and hyenas from her.

"Several weeks later, while I was scrounging for food, the men came quietly back to the village and caught me and several others. Jamal was the oldest among us, a teenager, who was immediately killed by the men without asking any questions or making any demands. He had a younger sister, whom the men took with them when they left the village—I never saw her again. Then, right after they killed Jamal, one of the boys that was with me pointed at me and said I was a Christian and I loved Jesus. One of the men said to the boy who pointed me out that he was a good Muslim. The other boys then joined in. They all betrayed me to save themselves. The men told me they would let me live if I agreed to become a Muslim. I said, 'No.' They told the other boys, if they really were good Muslims, to get a lot of wood and build a big fire, which they did. Then the men told the boys to throw me in the fire and keep me there with sharp sticks and clubs. At first, the boys didn't know what to do, so the men became angry and pushed me into the fire and said, 'See, like that. Now, keep him there if you're a good Muslim. Christians hate Allah, and Mohammed said to kill them!' I tried to escape but was beaten back. Someone hit me on the head with a rake, and I fell into the fire. I was still conscious, but the pain stopped.

"I could see a man in bright clothes coming toward me. He called my name, 'Philip, Philip,' and I got up and walked with him. He brought me here, and I've been here ever since. The Lord is good. He remembered a poor orphan boy, healed him, and gave him an honored place among his chosen people. Thank You, oh Lord my God, my Redeemer and Healer, my Master and Friend."

"Amen. The Lord is gracious and worthy of all praise," responds Karen.

"Amen," responds the group.

"Your story is so moving. But aren't you angry with God for letting your father and mother be killed and for letting you be killed like that?" asks Karen quietly and solemnly.

"It was man, not God, that killed my father and mother. And both my father and mother are here in Paradise, safe from harm, healed, redeemed, and praising God every moment of every day. No sister, from the human perspective, we blame God for things that are not His fault while we fail to thank Him for blessings and mercies we think we've earned on our own. Yet God is patient with us and accepts us lovingly when we turn to Him. God has shown us only good and has commended to us only love and life," says Philip the martyr.

"Why couldn't I see that? Why don't people see God's goodness and love?" asks Nora.

"In our humanness, our perceptions are dull and distorted. It takes strength and a willingness to face the truth about ourselves to begin to see God's goodness. Yet God's goodness is not something even angels can fully comprehend. I promise you one thing, my sister, that God's goodness will always amaze you no matter how long you know Him or how close to Him you abide," says Philip the martyr.

"Thank you, my brother Philip, for the hospitality and the lesson. I hope I've learned something. And may our good and merciful Lord smile upon you always. Amen," says Karen.

"Amen," responds the group. The ladies and the group depart as friends and go their own ways. The ladies both quietly contemplate the beauty and the faithfulness of Philip the martyr.

Chapter 29

"Nora, look up ahead. There's another big group gaining on us. They'll overtake us in a few minutes," says Karen.

"So, there is." Just then, AJ appears, walking with the ladies.

"This encounter should be interesting," AJ says.

"Who is it?" asks Nora.

"Thomas, the Lord's disciple," responds AJ.

"Thomas, the disciple. Wow! That's way cool," Karen exclaims.

"Yes, he's heading to the Library for a council meeting there. He's one of the highest-ranking people in Paradise. There is a standard protocol for interaction with people of such high rank," AJ says.

"Really, what is it, AJ?" Karen asks.

"Be respectful. That's all. Remember, people of Thomas's rank had, and continue to enjoy, special, personal, and continuous indirect access to the Lord."

"Thanks, AJ. I'll remember," responds Karen.

AJ calls out felicitations and greetings as the entourage overtakes the trio. "Hail, Thomas, the trustworthy disciple of the Lord!" An angel in Thomas's group responds, "Hail, fellow servants of the Most High."

"The Lord's peace be upon you. Will Thomas oblige his sisters and brother in brief discourse?" asks AJ. As soon as Thomas decides to fellowship with the trio, the grasses, flowers, and trees seem to magically reconfigure into a beautiful, living pavilion with comfortable benches. The ladies are in awe but remain silent.

"It would be our pleasure. I am Thomas, the Lord's most humble disciple; these are my worthy company of men and angels which the Lord has graciously provided to His servant."

"We are Nora, Karen, and Angel Jaynes," responds Nora. The group steps into the living pavilion as the introductions are made.

"Thomas, you're the famous disciple who actually walked with the Lord and said you would not believe the Lord was raised from the dead unless you saw with your own eyes and handled Him with your own hands," exclaims Nora.

"Yes, Nora, I am that Thomas, though I don't know anything about being famous, perhaps infamous. But I am not the subject of interest. The Lord is. His graciousness in allowing someone with such poor faith to abide with Him and continue as one of His favored few still humbles me profoundly. I had seen Him heal many blind and lame and even raise the dead. The Lord raised my former master's daughter from death! Yet, I wouldn't believe anyone's testimony that the Lord raised Himself from the dead. I look back on my unbelief now, and I'm aghast that I didn't even have the faith of a mustard seed, yet the Lord still loves me and invests in me. The Lord is good!"

"Amen," responds the company.

"What was He like, Thomas? What was it like to live with Him? Eat with Him and work with Him?" asks Karen.

Thomas looks up briefly and tears up. "It was so good. It was life. It was beauty. It was light and life. It was living-goodness just to be in His presence; it was incomparable sweetness just to hear Him speak. And when he healed someone, it was pandemonium! The joy in everyone exploded forth and seemed like it would last forever. But when he rebuked, it was fearful, so much so that no one could stand in His presence! Armed Temple guards would hide their faces in fear. Pharisees, Sadducees, and Scribes would be silent and turn their faces. There was, of course, never anyone like Him ever on the Earth, nor will there ever be again. But to be in His favor was peace, and beauty, and goodness. I don't know how else to describe it, but I long to be in His presence again more than anything else. To see Him, to hear Him, to abide with Him again, as I did before, I want nothing else. I'd give up my eternity to be in His presence for a day," Thomas says.

"Amen," solemnly responds the group.

"I can't wait to see Him. But I'm also afraid. He's so perfect and holy. I cannot stand in His presence," remarks Karen.

"No, my sister. None of us can, except by His grace and His righteousness. My brother and fellow disciple, John, whom the Lord loved so greatly, told me of the visions the Lord gave him while he was still on the Earth. He said that his vision of the Lord was so glorious that it terrified him, and he fell to his face on the ground like a dead man. But then the Lord spoke kindly to him, and he was able to stand in His presence. So, it is with all of us, even angels. Nothing alive or even inanimate could exist in His presence except by His grace toward us. So, it is good to fear the Lord, but remember that He loves you and will show you everlasting mercies and kindness when, at last, you appear before Him," Thomas says.

"Amen," solemnly responds the group.

The companions begin to kneel down facing Thomas, and Thomas urgently stops them. "Don't kneel to me, sisters. I am just your humble brother and fellow servant. Save your submission and thanksgiving for the Lord alone. And don't waste time as I did; love the Lord now, obey the Lord now, serve the Lord now, follow the Lord now. Don't wait for proof," Thomas concludes.

"Thank you, brother Thomas. Your wisdom is profound, and we will meditate upon it and do it. The Lord's goodness forever upon you, sir," declares Nora.

As the group walks away, the living pavilion reconfigures back into native flora, and Nora asks, "Why do you think Thomas had so little faith? Was his faith any less than the other disciples? Peter, John, and the rest of the disciples also ran. Perhaps Thomas had as much faith as they did. So, what was different about Thomas? Was he a former slave, an intellectual, or a teacher?"

"I don't know, but you ask interesting questions, Auntie Nora," Karen responds. "I think you're right that Thomas had as much faith as the other disciples. None of them exactly shined between the crucifixion and resurrection. So that probably means he simply couldn't believe what he himself did not directly observe."

"This brings up such a contrast," Nora says. "The women were faithful. And brave, even courageous."

"Yes, they were. In fact, the resurrected Lord first appeared to the women. What an honor!" Karen replies.

"And the disciples didn't believe the testimony of the women. It's not God who subjugates women; it's man. God gave women the greatest privilege in the universe, a privilege that can never be repeated; God has truly honored us," Nora proclaims.

"I see that now," responds Karen. "Thank You, Lord, blessed are You in my heart forever!"

"Well said, ladies," AJ says, "you've also brought me to tears. This is only the second time I've cried."

"And I bet this'll be the first time you've experienced a group hug," Karen says. "Bring it in. On me." And AJ experiences his first group hug; it's the third time he's cried.

After a brief interlude of worship through tears, the trio sees the growing expanse of the Library far off in the distance. "It must be enormous," remarks Nora.

"Aye, and beautiful, and always bustling with activity and learning. It's one of my favorite places in Paradise. You're almost there. Enjoy the rest of your travel. I'll take my leave now," says AJ.

"Before you do, AJ, please tell me about my family. How are they doing?" asks Karen. "All this beautiful emotion just reminded me that I have children and a husband."

"It's been about half an Earth year since your passing. Much has happened, most not good. Are you sure you want to burden yourself, Karen?"

"Yes, please, AJ, I must know how my family is doing. Although you frightened me when you said 'not good.'"

"Alright then, we'll have to stop in and visit them. I haven't been there for a little while. Look deeply into my face—"

As Karen softly perceives light, shadows, and silhouettes, she finally begins to see Roy. He's limping off the field toward the coach. She gasps with quickening excitement and joy, tears flowing, and her heart longingly explodes exponentially.

Chapter 30

"Don't worry 'bout it, Roy. You did good. Remember to keep your head up next time. Get some water and take a bench. I'll be calling you back in in a minute," instructs Coach.

AJ explains, "It's near the end of the third quarter, and the opposing team just took possession of the ball on their 20. The score is 13 to 7, other team's favor. Roy's never played defense, but one of the safeties is injured, and Coach wants to put Roy in the injured player's place."

"Roy!" yells Coach. "Get in there and take Right Safety."

"But, Coach, I—"

"Get in there!"

AJ continues, "Roy's taking Right Safety; he'll do his best. He's that kind of kid, but not a defensive player." Several minutes and plays later, AJ points out, "Oh, he just allowed a 'Hail Mary' to number 27 to clinch the win for the opposing team, but it seems the coach is proud of Roy's determination to do his best." The coach huddled the team, and AJ says, "The coach is debriefing the players on the field after the game, encouraging them and reassuring them that they're real football players practicing in the best traditions of the Little Hope Lions. Go, Lions!"

Karen observes the coach dismissing the players, and he calls Roy over to himself. "Help me with this equipment, son, and we'll get outta here."

"Yes, sir," says Roy.

As Coach drives Roy home, he rhetorically asks and answers, "Do you worry about your dad not making it to your games, Roy? He's a busy man. It doesn't mean he doesn't care. Know what I mean?" Roy is silent but briefly looks at the coach, then turns his head.

"I'm so sorry about your mother, Roy."

"It doesn't hurt anymore, Coach."

"Of course it does. And it will probably hurt all your life, son; I lost my kid sister about fifteen years ago to pancreatic cancer, and it still makes me cry when I think of her. Don't be afraid of the grief or the pain it causes. Deal with it like a man—don't give up, don't give in. Understand what I'm telling you?"

"Yes, sir. At least I think so, Coach."

"Many people lose heart and give up when the heat's on. They get beat by pain and take the easy way out. They blame God for their troubles and justify playing the victim. But people who give in are only fooling themselves. Bad things happen to all of us, kid, and what separates the men from the boys is how you deal with your circumstances when they happen to you. Life dealt you a tough hand, Roy, your mom's untimely death, and your dad's always off somewhere too busy for you and your needs, your pain. You don't deserve it, and I wish I could change it, but all I can do is encourage you and be your friend and your coach."

Roy gets tears in his eyes. He tries to turn his head so Coach won't see.

"What is it, Roy? And don't tell me 'nothing.'"

"I hate going home, Coach. Could I stay at your house?"

"What's wrong, Roy? Why do you hate going home?"

"My dad's always angry. He always yells at me."

"Has he ever hit you, Roy?"

"No, not really. But he scares me, and sometimes I'm afraid he's gonna hit me or something."

"God says we must honor our parents, but that doesn't mean we should allow them to abuse us. Wait a minute, let me think—"

The reality fades, and Karen begins to launch a protest through tears; as a new scene sharpens, Karen can start to make out Melody's form.

"Melody moved out of her home almost six months ago. She thought she was in love with Derek. She got pregnant and ran away to live with Derek. But when he found out that she was pregnant, he ended the relationship—if that's what you can call it. Melody got an abortion. Her son is in Paradise now; you'll get to meet him, Karen. She almost died from the chemical abortion, but a friend nursed her back to health. She repaid her friend by abusing the relationship, and eventually, she was evicted."

As Karen watches scenes in Melody's life play out, AJ continues, "Melody's now living with another friend, Yvette. At first, she was just going to crash with Yvette for a while, but Melody had nowhere else to go, and Yvette was not as patient as Linda was. Yvette insisted that Melody bring in some money right away—Melody had no prospects, so Yvette sent her to a club to dance. The club owner agreed to give her a try. The other girls told Melody the house rules, what to do, and how to do it. Melody makes some tips, and Yvette is satisfied for now. But Melody likes various drugs and unstable men."

Karen cries, "AJ, I need to help Melody—"

"Peace, Karen," AJ says. "I pray that the Almighty will send witnesses to her to intersect her and save her soul and life, but she has her own will, and God will not eclipse her will unless He's invited by her, or someone else, to do so." AJ prays. "When we return to Paradise, Karen, you won't remember any of these specifics about your loved ones. Just remember, trust God; He loves them even more than you do. He cries for them even more than you do. And He wants to give them life even more than you want them to have life and not death.”

"Thank you, AJ, but I'm not going back. I have to help Melody! I'm not going back! She needs me!”

"You won't remember anything in a moment,” AJ says. AJ guides her back to Paradise.

Part Four

The Library

Chapter 31

Karen and AJ return to Paradise. Karen is in hysterical tears. When Nora tries to comfort her, she is surprised to discover she has no recollection of why she's so upset. She just knows the terror is real down to the marrow. So, they somberly kneel, and each takes a turn praying for Karen. Finally, Karen's sobbing subsides, and the tenor of the supplication changes from petition to thanksgiving. Soon, the companions are singing worship songs. Karen interrupts the fellowship to thank the companions for their love and commitment.

"I'm so embarrassed," Karen softly says to her companions. "I don't know why I was so upset. I behaved like a silly girl."

"No, Karen," AJ responds, "we're on your side. Be at peace."

"We love you, Karen," Nora chimes in. "Nothing about you is silly."

And then Nora remembers the Library.

"I must confess, Karen, I've never been to the Library before. It seems I've been here such a short time. I've heard it's very beautiful, and I'm glad I get to see it for the first time with you," says Nora.

"Cool, tell me about it. Whatever you've heard," responds Karen as she intentionally drives herself back to a positive emotional frame.

"Of course, it has books, but not just books that are sitting on the shelves for reading, but books being continuously written by an army of angels," Nora says.

"Really? An army of angels are writing books? About what?" asks Karen.

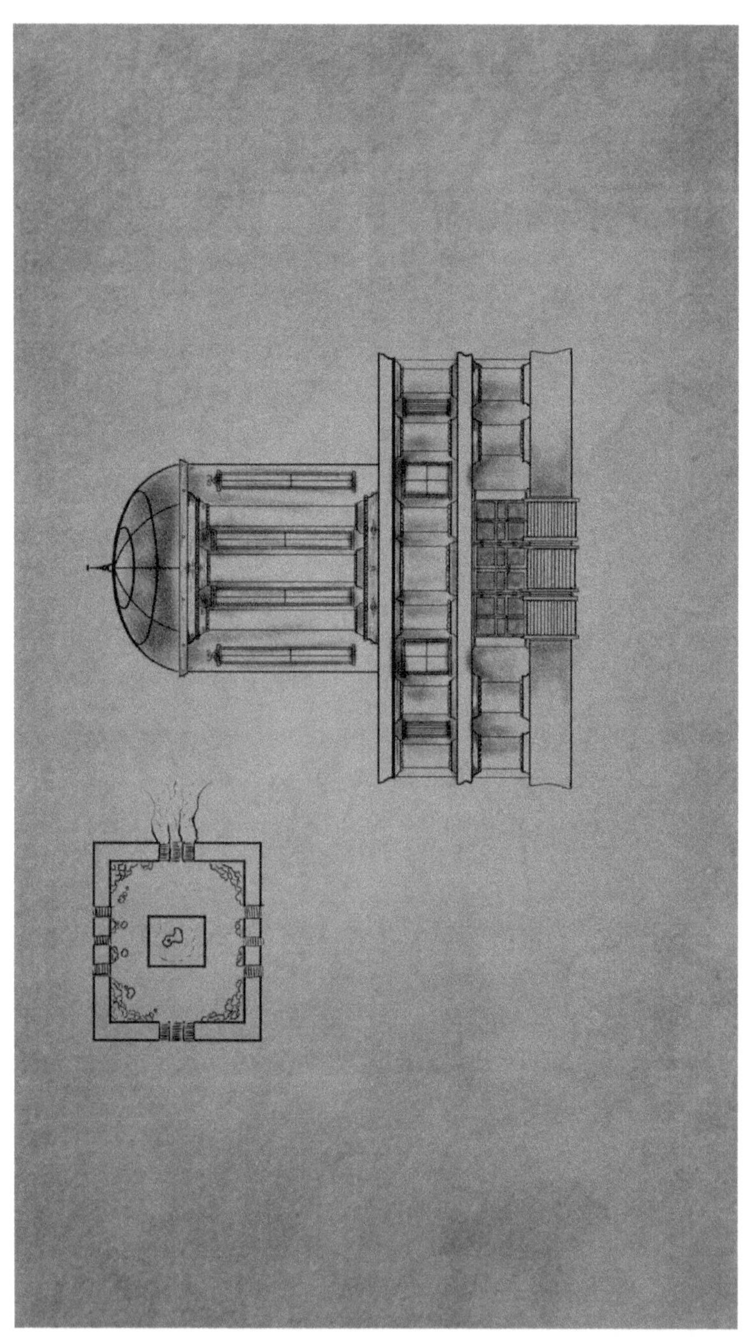

Figure 3 The Library

"I understand that they're writing the names and life histories of people now living—writing the events in their lives as they unfold. Is that right, AJ?" Nora asks.

"Yes, that's correct," AJ responds.

"How do they know what events are happening? And does that conflict with Free Will? And does that include everyone living and every single thing that happens, no matter how insignificant?" Karen asks.

"I'm not sure, Karen, we'll have to ask when we arrive. I'm sure we'll have many questions," responds AJ.

"I thought you knew everything, AJ," Karen says.

"No, there are many things in the Heavens that are on a need-to-know basis, and the special mission of the recording angels is considered secret as every entry is eternal and can only be expunged from the Books of Life at the command of God," says AJ.

The trio heads south-westward on Purity Path through the Rapturous Meadow toward the Library. They enter and depart several small towns and villages along the way. Each community consists of a few hundred to tens of thousands of souls.

The trio enters twin villages called Winsome and Handsome. Each is situated opposite the other on both sides of the road. Its name reflects the tenor of each village. The twin villages frequently gather as a single community to worship and fellowship. The trio is entering at the time of one of these celebrations.

"Greetings, beloved, to the Winsome-Handsome celebration," one of the greeters pronounces.

"You mean Handsome-Winsome celebration, don't you, sister?" remarks another greeter.

"And blessings of peace and well-being on your sojourn," cries one of the members of the Blessing Committee. "We're such a small community, we both greet and bless at the same time."

"Thank you for your welcome and blessing and good humor," says Nora. "What a lovely celebration. May we join in? And such friendly and lovely communities."

The trio introduces themselves and enters the celebration that extends from one village to the opposite end of the other village and encompasses the road. They first stop at a residence with a large and gorgeous garden, share some refreshments, and have a conversation in the village of Handsome. Then, they walk across the road to a family farm in the village of Winsome. A family farm here just means more than one resident. They spend some time harvesting corn, green beans, and strawberries, and discussing the pleasures of life in Paradise while working the fields. They fellowship with the family, enjoying the fruits (and vegetables) of their labors before continuing their journey.

A bit further down Purity Path, the trio encounters a medium-sized town: Abartee. This town is focused on martial arts, where humans train for their role in the Lord's Army. As they approach the town, the trio observes there's no Greeting Committee. Instead, there's a squad on either side of the road at ease and in their dress uniforms. An officer stands toward the end of one of the columns. The officer shouts, "Salute!" and the duty guards come to attention and salute the trio.

"This is a strange welcome," Nora says. "I don't quite know what to make of it."

"Abartee is a martial town, a special training outpost of recruits for the Lord's Army," AJ says.

"What's the purpose of the Lord's Army, AJ?" Nora asks. "Why does the Lord need an army? Is it for defensive or offensive purposes?"

"I don't know the precise answer. Presently, the army participates in ceremonial functions and trains. I do know there's going to be a battle. God will one day, whether in a single battle or an extended campaign, judge evil and execute punishment. I don't know the parameters of this judgment, nor does the army itself; all mission parameters are classified," AJ says.

The trio introduces themselves to the duty officer, who suggests that his commander may wish to meet them. The duty officer has the trio escorted to HQ. "General Baines, presenting Karen, Nora, and Angel Jaynes. Sir!" says the escort, Corporal Smitty.

"Welcome to Fort Nathanial here in beautiful downtown Abartee. My pleasure meeting you, favored children of God," greets General Baines.

"Thank you, General," replies Nora. "We don't know why we're being given such an honor, but it's appreciated, sir."

"I understand, from very high sources, that you were wondering about the Lord's Army, its purpose, and mission," says the general.

"We were, sir," responds Nora, "but we meant no impertinence, sir."

"My name's Merton; let's drop all the general stuff unless you want to enlist?"

"Oh no, sir, I mean Merton. I have no aptitude or desire to be a soldier," Nora says.

"That's fine, but let me know personally if you change your mind," replies Merton with a smile on his face. "So, where was I? Yes, I do not have authorization to answer your questions on the purpose or plans concerning the army. But I've been asked to share the answers to another related issue with you. Please have a seat, as this may take some time."

The trio sits on comfortable chairs in the general's office. "This topic concerns evil, and as you know, the legitimate purpose of any army is to confront and destroy evil. C. S. Lewis told the story in one of his fiction books with such exquisite articulation that I think it should be required reading for everyone; I'll just crudely paraphrase. In his book, God invites the occupants of Gehenna, the temporary place of torment for souls rejecting God, to Paradise. God's purpose was to give those condemned souls a final chance to repent and receive His mercy. In the story, every soul from Gehenna found Paradise painful and revolting and asked to be returned to Gehenna. Lewis unpacks this phenomenon by proposing, 'In the end, there are only two kinds of people, those who say to God, "Thy will be done," and those to whom God says, "Thy will be done."' The implication is that God is allowing each person their free will, that those in Gehenna choose to be there, and that they would find Paradise painful and undesirable. Lewis explained this by positing that those who reject God are becoming smaller, that is, less human, until they're a 'human residue.' This happens in a process where these self-centered folks become more and more self-centered, which is opposed to those who choose God—these folks become larger and larger as their concern for and love of others grows. Lewis reinforces Milton's proposition that 'It is better to rule in Heck than serve in Heaven.' Satan said that he is entirely self-focused. Thus, for Milton and Lewis, the damned choose to grow smaller and less human by increasing self-focus, but the saved grow larger and more godly by growing in their love for God and others," says the general.

"I see the logic of the proposition," says Nora, "but I thought people are saved by the Lord's atonement alone."

"This is true. God could forgive no one without the atonement. Atonement is both necessary and sufficient for complete salvation for any and all. The issue is, some don't want salvation because they don't want God; they want to be their own god," says the general.

"What a pathetic and horrid thought!" responds Nora.

"Indeed," responds the general, "so to wrap this up, the army will engage evil and defeat it, but evil exists to give people freedom of choice: God is God, or we are god. The God is God folks are growing in godliness, becoming larger and developing into the image of His Son. We are our own god folks reject God, and they grow smaller as their self-focus increases until they become a mere human residue."

As the trio takes their leave, they continue toward the Library. "My goodness, this Library keeps getting bigger and bigger. It practically fills the horizon," Karen comments.

"Yes, and we're still some distance," replies AJ.

"No question it can hold at least one army, if not several. What else can you tell us about the Library, AJ?" asks Karen.

"Just that it's an important center of authority in Paradise. Each city has its own governing council and, of course, its own Archangel. Each city is the center of authority for one of God's major missions. But the Library does have a special mission related to the recording angels, which I won't tell you about. You'll have to discover it for yourselves," says AJ.

"Very cool; let's find out what it is!" Karen says.

"Deal!" responds Nora.

As the trio approaches the Library from the East, they can see three roads converging toward three gigantic entrances on the eastern face of the Library. While still some distance away, they can see at least one road leading to the Library entrances on the eastern and northern faces. However, the distances are significant, and they can't tell from their vantage point that there are a total of twelve entrances, three on each face of the Library, each with its own road. The Library sits in the approximate middle of the Rapturous Meadow, a huge section of gently rolling hills covered in moderately tall grasses and wildflowers with occasional clusters of trees. The colors of the flowers span the spectrum from reds and yellows to browns and blues on an opulence of greens. The smells and sounds are equally wonderful and diverse. As they continue toward the entrance, the scale of the Library is so immense that they can no longer see the roads leading to the other sides, and they can barely discern the top of the structure, but they can begin to make out some writing carved into a large plate above the entrance they're approaching. When they're close enough to read the writing above the entrance, Nora reads it out loud, "Wonderful Counselor."

The trio continues along the road, occasionally stopping and engaging in polite conversation with others coming and going. Finally, they reach the end of the road and negotiate the 144 marble steps organized into twelve flights of twelve steps each. At the top of each flight is a large landing or patio. The roof of the portico extends over the top of the final flight of steps, supported by a colonnade of massive columns that appear to be made of multicolor onyx. The base of each column seems to be approximately fifty people standing shoulder-to-shoulder in diameter. The columns are so high that the size of the capitals can't be accurately estimated. The ladies are told that there are five columns on each face of the Library, three entrances on each face, the main entrance, and two smaller ones. The name of the east-face entrance is Wonderful Counselor. The names of the other three main entrances are Mighty God on the north face, Everlasting Father on the west, and Prince of Peace on the south.

"We're entering the Wonderful Counselor Gate. The Lord is indeed our Wonderful Counselor," Nora says.

"Amen," responds Karen. "There must be hundreds of people entering and leaving the Library through just this one entrance every minute. This patio floor seems to be some kind of quartz. And the stone is not cold to the touch."

"And it has a wonderful aroma," Nora says, "like a flower. I never thought a stone could smell good."

"Every time I think to myself that nothing can surpass the beauty and awesomeness I'm presently enjoying, the next step or corner or minute brings something even more wonderful," Karen says.

"Amen, sister," Nora says. "I'm sorry I've never visited the Library 'til now. It was always on my list, and many others told me to go enjoy it, but I was in too much delight-of-the-moment to tear myself away from whatever else I was presently involved with."

"Look at these windows, Nora," Karen says.

"The windows are about five hundred feet tall, and the glass is about ten feet thick, but it's so perfectly clear that there's no image distortion," remarks AJ. "If you look closely, you'll see that the glass is water, and fish and various aquatic lifeforms are swimming within the 'glass.' The door frames are jasper if I know my semi-precious stones."

"How does He do that?" asks Karen and Nora. "Is it glass or water?"

"How does He do anything? It's all a mystery and miracle to me," AJ responds.

"But how do the fish eat? What do they eat?" asks Karen.

"Nothing eats anything in Paradise," AJ responds. "The fish have no need even as you have no need, but you eat for fellowship and enjoyment of God's bounty. But nothing dies when you or we eat in Paradise."

"Do you mean the vegetarians were right?" asks Karen.

"More or less, but on Earth, God provided plants and animals for human consumption; in Paradise, no creature needs to replenish their energy supply."

"That makes me so happy, AJ! Thank You, Lord!" exclaims Karen.

"I'm not as happy about it as you are, Karen my dear. I used to enjoy a good ribeye," Nora says.

The excitement grows as the trio moves close enough to the entrance to touch one of the open doors. The doors appear to be made of solid gold, at least five feet thick and hundreds of feet high. The doorframes are blood-red ruby. A contingent of people and angels greet those entering the Library, saying, "Enter by the Blood and abide brethren."

Once inside, AJ takes his leave to catch up on some reading; the trio agrees to reconvene near the center of the Library, on the first floor by the lake, after sufficient time to explore and read. The ladies see thousands of people and angels standing, sitting, reading, discussing, worshipping, and browsing books. There are many tables, couches, and other accommodations for sitting alone or in small or large groups. There are many rooms along the periphery and in large bulkheads within the vast expanse of the inner space. The first-floor ceiling appears several sub-stories up and is decorated with beautiful reliefs.

The ladies take their time to explore the architecture and observe that the interior walls are made of pearls of various shades, from white to platinum to peach, to gold, to brown to black. They can see the intricate designs carved deep into the pearl—trees, fruit, and animals. The ceiling (on this floor and in this section) has crown molding with carved designs, and the flat sections have paintings and other geometric reliefs.

Some of the windows show a view of the grand meadow outside and stained-glass graphics. Scenes of the Lord's heavenly and earthly ministries carved into reliefs situated in regular patterns, earmarking boundaries of massive sections on this floor of the Library, can be seen as the trio proceeds toward the center of the Library. The first one is of His birth in Bethlehem. The ladies notice the delightful scent of balsam as they pass this relief. The next was of His baptism by John, and the scent was like cedar. The ladies saw several other scenes and smelled sandalwood, the sea, and rosewood aromas. Aromas of Frankincense and Myrrh accompanied the crucifixion scene. Hundreds of souls and angels in solemn states of awe were crying and worshipping at this scene. After some unknowable amount of time, the ladies turn toward each other and see that they've both been in deep, tearful worship.

As the ladies continue toward the center of the Library, they observe a brightness that appears to be emanating from the ceiling ahead of them. A vast domain opens above them, so large that they cannot make out the boundaries in any direction. They do see that several mammoth lofts extend to what may be the width of the opening above them, and there appear to be many angels working on the lofts. They make their way parallel along the width of the loft directly above them to appreciate the scale better. They discover that other lofts at different vertical levels in the expanse are above the ones they've been following. The reason is that this vast open space contains many massive lofts connected to the periphery of the expanse along all four sides and that this must be the approximate center of the Library.

"The angels working on each level of the lofts must have something to do with the purpose of the Library," says Nora.

"Yes, of course," replies Karen.

Twelve columns form a colonnade on the outside aspect on each side of the opening so that the lofts are cantilevered toward the exterior on each face of the vast expanse so that there is a gap between the Library interior bulwarks and the lofts.

"How do the angels get to the lofts when there's a large gap? There's no pathway," asks Karen.

"We'll have to ask AJ. I have no clue," responds Nora.

The ladies observe a tranquil lake on the main floor extending under much of the open space. Angels and people alike walk on the surface of the lake to one of several small islands or just to enjoy walking on the water. The interior is so large that one's perception is that they are out-of-doors, as there's a huge skylight letting in much sunshine at the top of the opening.

"Let's go walk on water!" Karen exudes.

"Last one there's a monkey's uncle!" retorts Nora. But on their way to the lake, they see an interesting person. So, they stop to talk briefly.

"Pardon me, sir. My name is Karen, and this is my buddy Nora."

"Pleased to meet you, Karen, Nora. My name is Sam. How may I be of service?"

"This is our first time at the Library. What is the name of this lake, and what is its function, please?" asks Karen.

"My, you're curious for a human. Most unnatural," quips Sam.

"Lord of the Rings! Gandolf to Frodo," says Karen.

"Right you are, I love JRR Tolkien's works. He's here in Paradise. Perhaps you'll get to meet him. The lake is named Bethesda. It's a place of healing, rest, and quiet. People and angels visit here occasionally to soak in its beauty and peace. If you want to experience it, just go to the shoreline and step onto the water. I'll be happy to show you if you like," says Sam.

"Thanks, Sam, I would like that. Nora, are you game?"

"Of course, I wouldn't miss this for anything," responds Nora.

"Okay, then follow me right over here. Now, when you step onto the water for the first time, you may feel a little uncertain," says Sam.

"How deep is it? Is it slippery?" asks Karen. "I never could skate."

"Don't worry, just remember who you belong to and trust Him," responds Sam.

AJ sneaks up on Karen from another section of the Library.

Chapter 32

"Karen," AJ says, trying to look stern, "there's no squealing in Paradise, especially in the Library."

"Ah, you're back, AJ. This place is great! Okay, here goes." (A few moments go by, trying to step onto the lake.) "Wow, this is wild! Nora, you've got to try this! I'm walking on water!"

"Bless me! I'm doing it too. This is so fun; I never thought I'd be doing anything so exciting. God is so good to us!" shouts Nora.

"Amen!" is Karen and Sam's response.

"Let's play Jesus walking on the water. I'll be Jesus, you're Peter," Karen directs.

"I'll be Peter, just remember to save me!" replies Nora. The ladies have fun playing Jesus and Peter in the storm; it appeared more than once that Jesus may have been a bit slow to rescue Peter.

"Sam, how do you get to one of these lofts overhead?" asks Nora.

"I'm sorry, sister; you can't. The lofts are for angels only. That's where they do their work; the angels are commissioned to write the Book of Life. That's why there's a distance gap between the lofts and the Library's bulkheads, so humans can't get over there. There is quite literally an army of angels ceaselessly writing the names and deeds of people into the books," says Sam.

"The Book of Life? What's that, Sam?" asks Karen.

"The Book of Life is the record our Holy God will use to judge the living and the dead. If a person's name is found in the Book of Life, he belongs to God. If not, then he does not belong to God. So, you see, this is a very important task, and it is God's domain, not man's, so we're not permitted access to these records nor to even watch the angels write, up close that is," says Sam.

"And you said something about the deeds of people; what's that?" Karen asks.

"I don't know for sure. I've always figured it must be each person's important thoughts, feelings, actions, and inactions while on Earth. AJ would know better than me," says Sam.

"You're correct, Sam," AJ says. "But the deeds refer to the effects, not the causes. That is, souls express who they are in their behaviors. But a person's behavior doesn't define him or her; the soul's relationship to God Almighty is the cause, and the behaviors are the effect. That doesn't mean that a person's behaviors aren't important to God, but rather that they are only indicators of a person's spiritual condition, which is firmly rooted in their relationship to God."

"I see. Thanks, AJ," Sam says, then turning to the trio, he continues, "You've been most kind to take time with me. May our Lord richly bless you, Karen, Nora, and AJ."

"You're so welcome, Sam. The Lord already has, and may He continue to bless you and yours," says Karen.

AJ indicates he just received a message, politely takes his leave, and returns to Earth.

Chapter 33

AJ materializes at the Hill's house, in the hall leading to the bathroom. He can hear Roy speaking to himself in the bathroom behind the closed door. "I'm really proud of you, son. You're a real hero to the team and the school … And what's this? (closely examining his chin, he believes he spots what might be the beginnings of a single microscopic hair) A beard! O' yeah!" Roy feels a hunger pang; it's about 6:30 p.m. Bert and Margareta haven't come home yet, so Roy will have to kluge something up in the kitchen again (the church stopped delivering dinners since Bert's outburst, the pastor fearing Bert's instability could put someone in danger).

"Let's see. A hot dog bun, ketchup, and, ah, cheese. Sounds good." After supper preparation, he sits up and says, "Lord, thank you for the food, school, and soccer. Please help my dad, so he's not angry all the time. And please take care of my mom. She's been in Heaven for a long time. Please give her some friends so she's not lonely. Please protect Melody. I don't know where she is, and I kinda miss her."

After supper, Roy goes to his room and completes his homework. The algebra homework is due tomorrow, and Roy suspects the teacher will give a pop quiz, so he's diligent (his bedroom door remains open). Roy's afraid to turn on the TV, so he listens to the radio in his room. He toggles between his favorite rock 'n roll station and a Christian station he found one day when he was in deep despair, almost like maybe someone answered an urgent prayer for safety and comfort. He falls asleep about 9 p.m., and Bert and Margarita have still not come home.

***

The next day, Roy meets the bus down the block and heads off to school. After school is soccer practice. It's spring, and the soccer season's about to spin up. Coach Binder recommended to Roy that he try soccer, to which Roy was amenable. Coach Tapri, the soccer coach, assembles the boys in a hard-to-understand dialect and offers up a prayer for the boys' safety and for God to make Himself and His love for each of the boys evident in their lives. Then, he orders them to their starting positions for drills.

After the day's practice and a brief scrimmage, Roy approaches the coach and asks, "Where are you from, Coach?"

"Why do you ask me that, Roy? I'm an American."

"I'm sorry, Coach. I didn't mean any disrespect. Mrs. Grant, my World Culture teacher, said that Indians from India are Hindu. But you're a Christian. And you talk with an accent, so you're real confusing to me."

"I am from India, Roy. I'm from the Kinnaur District. I was born there, but my parents moved to the U.S. in 1970 when I was a kid. And I am a Christian. My parents are Christians. They were converted by missionaries in India before we immigrated. I became a Christian afterward. And as far as the accent goes, I have no idea what you're talking about. You better open up your ears."

"Sorry, Coach. Just one more thing: I hate to bring it up, but I think you should know. During drills, I heard Mitch say to one of the other players that he and his parents are atheists, and when he tells his parents that you pray with the team, his parents will complain to the principal and the school board."

"Complain to the principal?" Coach asks.

"Well, that's not what Mitch said exactly, but that's what he meant. I can't say exactly what Mitch said 'cause it's wrong to use that kind of language."

"I see. Thanks for letting me know, Roy. But I don't worry about such things. I've been brought before the board several times, but I trust God to expose the truth and uphold His honor." Coach puts his arm around Roy's shoulder. "Roy, Coach Binder told me about you. He said you were a real winner."

"Really?" asks Roy.

"Yes, really. And he also said that you lost your mother about a year ago. I'm so sorry, Roy."

"That's okay, Coach. But it was seven months ago," Roy says.

"Coach Binder told me that you go to church pretty regularly. Do you know the Lord as your Savior, Roy?" Coach asks.

"I don't know what you mean, Coach," responds Roy.

"How does one become a Christian, Roy?"

"You go to church and believe in God. Isn't that right?"

"It's partially right but not completely. You see, there are plenty of people who go to church that don't belong to God, and there are plenty of people that don't go to church that do," Coach says.

"Why don't they belong to God, Coach?" asks Roy.

"Because they belong to themselves," replies Coach.

"I don't understand, Coach," Roy says.

"If you belong to yourself, that is, if you maintain ownership of yourself, your rights, your wants, your desires, your will, then you don't belong to God. When we give up our ownership of ourselves to God, then God owns us. We belong to God from that point forward. It's what some Christians call 'accepting Jesus Christ as Lord and Savior.'"

"I still don't understand, Coach. I'm sorry, I must be stupid."

"Don't ever say that. You're smart, just the way God designed you. And this isn't something that we can just grasp with our minds. It's something that we acquire with our hearts. You see, God is a God of love and justice. He loves us, each of us. He created us, and He wants a relationship with us. But because we sin and He is holy, He can't have a relationship with us. God can't look upon sin, and sin can't be in God's presence because He's sinless, perfect, and pure. God, in His justice, said that the penalty for sin is death and that sin has to be paid for—in full. So, God must destroy sin, but to destroy sin means destroying the people He loves. So, God decided to pay the penalty for sin Himself. That's why Jesus was born into the world— to pay the death sentence for sin, my death sentence, and your death sentence, the death sentence of everyone who believes. That's why Christ had to die so that we could live. And if we believe this, Jesus becomes our Lord and our Savior."

"Wow. I never heard it explained that way. I knew Jesus died on the cross, but I didn't understand why until now," Roy says.

"Now that you understand God has love for you, Roy, are you ready to accept God's gift of forgiveness of your sins and eternal life with Him?"

"Yes. Yes, I am." Roy turns his attention upward. "Thank You, Jesus. I accept Your gift and ask You to be my Savior and Lord," Roy prays.

"*Hallelujah*! Congratulations, Roy, you're a Christian. Tell your family. And then your next step is to get baptized ..."

Coach went on to explain about Believer's Baptism, and Roy ran home joyfully and enthusiastically like he hadn't experienced in years. He thought about whom he might tell but didn't have anyone he could think of except Coach Binder.

AJ returns to Paradise.

Chapter 34

Nora noticed a gentleman looking at them as they were walking on the water and following them with an intense gaze. "That man over there, along the beach in that rainbow of colors," reports Nora.

"Yes, I see him," responds Karen.

"He's been looking at us pretty intently," says Nora.

"Is that an easel? I bet he's an artist. Let's go see!"

Karen bolts toward the man and dashes to the front of the easel to view the canvas. "Oh my, it's gorgeous. It's moving! I've never seen a moving painting before—it's alive!" remarks Karen in utter excitement.

"And whom do I have the pleasure of speaking with, sister?" asks the artist.

"I'm sorry, my name is Karen, this is my buddy Nora. We're related."

"Yes, child, we're all related here. And I'm Claude. I've been painting Peace Isle for some time and saw you two walking on the water and playing like young souls, so I added you to the painting. Here you are, see?"

"Ah, that's you, Karen, and this must be me," says Nora.

"Yes, that's right," says Claude.

"It looks like we're dancing; it's beautiful—the painting's actually moving. And look, I seem to be changing color. It looks like I'm going back and forth between happy and distressed," says Karen.

"No, it can't be that," responds Nora to Karen as she turns with a questioning look on her face to Claude. "Can it?"

"That's how it appears. I don't necessarily understand what I paint; I just paint what I feel. But in your case, my dear, it appears you have something weighing on you or is about to."

"I feel delighted and secure, but I don't deserve it. At times, I bear a penetrating grief and unrelenting guilt about something, but I have no idea what."

"Sister, I just got this urge of excitement pass over me as you were lamenting. Our good Lord is about to do something wonderful for you, and I don't understand what or how, but apparently, I'm supposed to be part of it," explains Claude as he begins to put his paints up and fold his easel.

"Really?" asks Karen.

"Really?" asks Nora. "No way, you're no more than twelve."

"Really, and so I should probably introduce myself. I'm Claude Monet, a humble painter for the King of Beauty. As for my demeanor, I'm exactly as the Lord wants me."

"The Claude Monet? The great French Impressionist?" asks Karen.

"Not so great, my sister. I'm honored beyond my worth. To be the least apprentice in the lowest trade serving our Lord would satisfy me beyond all gratitude I could bear. But I was an Impressionist with several friends and colleagues; perhaps you heard of Renoir, Degas, and Cézanne?" asks Claude.

"Of course, Monsieur Monet," responds Nora. "I've always loved your work. But this kind of living painting you do now is beyond anything I've ever seen. How do you do it?"

"I don't know, but neither do I know how not to paint in this way. It just comes; I can't help it or control it. It just comes. But please, sisters, call me Claude."

"Claude, I don't know how you can help me, but Nora and I welcome you into our company, and we submit ourselves to God's wisdom and will. And thank you in advance for your support, whatever and whenever that will be."

"Karen, Nora, let's go find some books!" exclaims Claude. "I want to learn about adventures. We're about to embark on one."

"We'll need to start by discovering how the Library is organized. There must be billions of books here," remarks Nora.

The three find a librarian who further instructs them in the layout and use of the Library. They decide to secure a book on the flora and fauna of Paradise. There are three copies of the text on the shelf and comfy chairs side by side for reading. As they quietly and interactively read the books, AJ appears at a short distance and walks quickly over to the friends.

"I've got some exciting news for you both. And, Claude, hello, it's been a while. What are you currently painting?" asks AJ.

Nora says, "This is Claude Monet, the great French Impressionist painter! But it sounds like you both already have met. Claude will be joining our fellowship."

"Welcome to the fellowship, Claude. We are most pleased to share your company," responds AJ.

"So, what's the good news, AJ?" asks Karen.

"Michael, the Archangel, is coming to the Library in moments. He's coming for a council meeting. I don't know who else is supposed to be attending or what the subject is, but seeing Michael will be fascinating. Karen, I know this will be your first Archangel experience. Nora, have you ever seen an Archangel before?"

"No, I haven't. What's an Archangel? How is he different from you?" asks Nora.

"Archangels are the greatest of all angels. There are seven, and they each stand in the very presence of God. And each Archangel is the chief executive of his organization or operation for God. There are several levels of hierarchy between an angel such as myself and an Archangel, and we lower angels rarely, if ever, stand directly in the presence of the Almighty."

"You sound almost as excited to see Michael as we are, AJ."

"I am; it's such a wonderful thing. Oh, I forgot momentarily. In all my excitement, you may not actually be able to see Michael. He'll be here, but a human soul must be of a certain spiritual maturity level to be able to see and experience an Archangel. You may just see a blinding light and feel an overwhelming power." AJ turns toward Claude. "Have you ever seen Michael, Claude?"

"I've had the honor of experiencing Michael on one previous occasion."

"What's the protocol for meeting an Archangel, AJ?" asks Nora.

"There is a formal protocol, but you won't need to know it this time. You won't actually get to meet Michael. But you may be able to observe that a reception committee will form at the welcome location. Then, before Michael arrives, a herald will precede and announce him. An honor detachment will accompany Michael and escort him to the place of welcome. The reception committee will formally welcome him, and then he'll be escorted to the high council chambers for his meeting."

"It sounds terribly exciting, AJ," remarks Claude. "When I had the pleasure of seeing Michael previously, from a distance, of course, I couldn't make out his form exactly. It was like the coalescence of palpable beauty and immeasurable strength. I don't know how else to explain it."

"That's about as good an explanation as anyone could give of Michael."

"This is a rare occurrence. I'm so pleased you'll be experiencing it. Look, over there, the reception committee is forming on Peace Isle.

Angel Ur, the head curator of the Library, and the senior staff angels along with the human elders, including Charles Spurgeon, the very large-looking elder, and Oswald Chambers are assembling," says AJ.

"Oh, I always loved their devotionals. Many of their writings made me cry. Could we meet them?" asks Nora.

"I'm sure it can be arranged, but not until sometime after the high council meeting," responds AJ.

Just then, some commotion on Peace Isle is observed, and the Archangel's herald appears. All eyes are on this marvelous being dressed in a bold red robe with much luminous gold armor. The herald announces the arrival of the Archangel Michael in a loud voice, which the fellowship cannot understand, and then the honor detachment appears and stands at attention (the honor detachment consists of seven high-ranking angels likewise dressed in red with gold armor). Then Michael appears as a radiant ball of fire, like a miniature sun, so bright that all the ladies can see is blinding whiteness, no matter which direction they turn their heads. They immediately feel a deep rumbling power, like they are standing next to the space shuttle as it is taking off. They can smell a savory aroma, not sweet but pleasant. Then, as quickly as it began, it is over. AJ explains to the ladies that Michael made a few polite remarks to the people and angels gathered to welcome him, and then the reception committee escorted him to the high council chambers. Just then, the ladies can discern the shouts of praises to God and blessing on the commander of His hosts as the deep rumbling power fades. Shortly after that, their sight starts to recover.

"What did we just experience, AJ? It was like an altered reality," asks Nora.

"Just as Einstein theorized that massive gravity can distort space and time, so massive spiritual energy can distort reality. An Archangel's holiness must be immense to be able to stand in the presence of the Almighty. And even though it is, they could not stand in His presence without the benefit of His grace and mercy. God's holiness and power are unknowable, to human or angel, and it's more awesome and fearful than I can even relate. (a brief moment of silence) Praise and honor be to our God, most holy and kind," pronounces AJ.

"Amen," is the solemn response.

"AJ, what does 'the commander of His hosts' mean exactly?" asks Nora.

"The Archangel Michael is the Commander, or General, of God's armies, Heaven's Hosts. The Lord Himself is the Commander-In-Chief, but the Lord leads his vast armies through Michael," says AJ.

"Did you see Michael's ceremonial sword? I was simultaneously terrified and awestruck," remarks Claude.

"You could actually see Michael? Your spiritual age appears no older than Nora's and mine," asks Karen. "What does it mean, AJ? I don't understand. I thought it required spiritual maturity to see an Archangel; perhaps it's his childlike innocence. I remember from the Scripture that the Lord said we '… must be like little children to enter the Kingdom of Heaven.'"

"Ah, yes, but that's a slight misunderstanding of what the Lord meant. He was referring to a person's status as a child of God; only adopted children of God enter Heaven. He wasn't referring to innocence or childishness," answers AJ.

"I see. Thanks, AJ," responds Karen.

"Your spiritual age is only one dimension of your relationship with God, but there are many, and it's not the same between the Almighty and all persons. Love, faithfulness, and devotion represent living relationship dimensions; other dimensions include fidelity and purity. It so happens that Claude's love and purity dimensions are developed very greatly—perhaps, as an artist, he was a man after

God's own heart—but Claude needs to develop other dimensions, which he's reluctant to do. Isn't that right, Claude?" asks AJ.

"I live in the reality I choose. It may seem selfish to some, but I refuse to bow to objective reality. If I experience something objectionable, I fix it in my heart and my expressions of art. I inhabit a world that should be, not a world that is," explains Claude.

"I see, interesting, Claude. I respect your view and agree with it. But don't you mean you fix it in your mind?" asks Nora.

"The mind, certainly not. The heart is the seat of humanity and divine love, not the mind. The mind is deceitful and manipulative; never trust it," responds Claude.

"What did you mean by living dimensions, AJ?" asks Karen.

"The Almighty is life, and any relationship with Him is alive. However, sin has corrupted creation, so God is re-making all things, making all things new. When this work is complete, all relationships will be alive and perfect overall dimensions," says AJ.

"I thought the Lord's work on the cross was complete. What are you saying, AJ?" asks Nora.

"The Lord's redeeming work of atonement for the payment of sin was completed on the tree. But salvation has past, present, and future components in the lives of human beings," remarks AJ.

"What do you mean salvation has past, present, and future aspects?" asks Nora.

"2 Cor 1:10–11 are two verses that express this well: a past, present, and future tense of His redemptive work all in two adjoining verses. Other scriptures express these three tenses as well. The point is that a person's salvation was, is, and is to come. With respect to the Scripture cited, He delivered, He delivers, and He will deliver; past, present, and future."

"How does this apply specifically to people, AJ?" asks Nora.

"When a person is introduced to the Lord Jesus, He makes a claim on their lives and offers His free gift of salvation. If a person accepts the Lord's claim and the free gift, a covenant transaction occurs, and the person is adopted into God's Family to enjoy all the benefits thereof: forgiveness of their sin debt and the right to a relationship with the Almighty. In this sense, salvation is a past fact; it's a done deal since the atonement is complete. But God loves His children too much to leave them as they are. That is, He doesn't just forgive our sins, but he's expunging our sinful nature from us. Imagine how miserable we would be in Heaven, in God's presence, and how miserable God would be if we were just forgiven for our sins but still bore a sinful nature. So, salvation must be more than just mere forgiveness. Thus, He continues to work with His children to sanctify them, and they're given the privilege to be coworkers with God in the redemption of His creation in cooperating with the Holy Spirit. In this way, salvation is a continuing sanctifying process. Finally, God will translate all those that belong to Him into the perfect image of His Son. This is a future aspect of salvation when man will be made perfect and eternally incorruptible; only as eternally perfect and incorruptible beings can humankind abide in God's presence," concludes AJ.

The companions fall to their knees and solemnly worship the Lord. "Righteous and true are Your judgments, oh Lord; magnificent and awesome are You alone!"

Slowly, the functions and operations of the Library resume along their usual path without direct observation by the companions. Then Karen asks, "Would you please update me on my family, AJ? I have loved ones on Earth but know nothing about them."

AJ indicates he needs to revisit them and will update Karen when he returns.

Chapter 35

It's been about an Earth week since AJ's last visit to the Hill household. Bert and Margareta come home for dinner. Roy perceives that Bert's in about as good a mood as he's been in recent history, so he decides to tell him that he's become a Christian about a week ago and wants to get baptized. Unfortunately for Roy, he doesn't see the malicious demon speaking to Bert, guiding, directing, agitating. "Finally I have some peace, nothing's gonna ruin tonight. Tonight's my night. The world can rot as far as I'm concerned …" barks Poison, the demon.

"Dad, I just became a Christian! I gave my life to Jesus! Can I get baptiz—"

"What? What the heck are you talking about, Christian? I've had enough of those hypocrites! They tell you 'God loves you' on one hand, then God stabs you in the back when you're not looking!"

"Bert, that's not right," said Margareta.

"The heck it isn't! Well, I want no part of it. You do what you want; it's your life to ruin."

"I think it's a fine thing, Roy. But I don't understand. Your parents were both Christians, weren't you already baptized?" asks Margareta.

"I don't kno—" Roy tries to say.

"Yes, he was baptized a few weeks after he was born. His mother wanted it."

"See, you were baptized, Roy, so you don't need to get baptized again," says Margareta.

"But the Bible says—" Roy again tries to speak.

"The Bible says! Enough of all that. I want to enjoy my dinner in peace. You do what you want. But don't come running back to me, I warned ya!"

AJ leans over toward Roy and whispers in his ear: "Yes! Good man, Roy," which he cannot hear, but somehow, he perceives the boon and takes it as encouragement.

***

Roy asked Coach Tapri to perform the baptism. Coach asks if Roy's dad wants to do it. Roy informs Coach that Bert wants no part of it, so Coach consents. Roy informs his youth group leader of his decision and desire to be baptized. He learns he and whoever baptizes him must attend a short baptism class. Roy informs Coach about the class, and Coach says he's game. They attend the baptism class one Wednesday evening and set the date for the baptism.

Roy's baptism was conducted by Coach Tapri at Roy's church one Sunday after the second service. There was a brief reception afterward for all those baptized that day with refreshments and lots of conversation. Coach drove Roy home, and brought up Roy's sister. Roy says she hates him, and that's why she never calls or comes by the house to see how he's doing. "I needed her so many times, but she just wasn't there." Coach tries reassuring Roy that Melody doesn't hate him; he can't explain her behavior, but he's sure she doesn't.

AJ decides to visit Melody. Crescenda got tired of *dancing* and all the sexual pressure constantly on her from her boss, Tony 'the Duke,' and the customers. So, she quit and started to work odd jobs, holding them for one to two months before getting fired, usually for missing work or coming into work drunk or stoned. She's frequently late for work, not properly attired, and often full of excuses. She occasionally sleeps with her bosses to retain her job. If she didn't, her jobs would last a couple of weeks rather than months.

She hangs out with several young men, but her main squeeze, Tough Nuts, is a petty dealer with high ambitions of owning the city. He turns her on to meth and crack. She can't pay him for all the drugs, so he makes her turn tricks on the side (with other dealers to help Tough Nuts' network; she does not consider this to be prostitution). Crescenda eats poorly and has gained weight (no nutrition, just empty calories). Tough Nuts one night, after a failed deal, comes back to the crib in a violent mood, and when he sees Crescenda asleep on the floor with the TV blaring and food spilled on the carpet beside her, he beats her for being fat and lazy and then kicks her out of the apartment. Crying and out on the street, in pain from a busted lip and a black eye, she has a brief thought of her brother Roy, but a demon is speaking to her and defocuses her thoughts of Roy.

Crescenda, staggering on the street, sees a young woman she knows, Crystal, and they get to talking. Crystal says she's done her quota for the night and invites Crescenda to crash at her apartment. Crescenda has no place to go at this time of night, so she agrees. This devolves into Crescenda's first lesbian encounter. The morning after, Crescenda is horrified at what she's done and runs out of Crystal's apartment back to the streets. She spends the day looking up friends she might be able to stay with. She finds none and returns to Crystal after being unable to turn any tricks or get even one fix.

Several weeks later, Crescenda gets busted for petty possession. She spends a week in jail and is let go due to overcrowding. After being released, Crescenda walks past a group of women picketing an abortion center. One of the women recognizes her disheveled state and strikes up a conversation. "Don't you know that God loves you? Don't you know that Jesus died for your sins and wants to make you clean and give you new life?" However, Crescenda immediately and spontaneously rejects the Gospel and prefers denial and the trash of the streets. A demon accompanies Crescenda all the time now, blinding her to the Gospel. The demon laughs at Crescenda's plight as she walks away. "You're mine, you're mine, give up, you're mine—" it says.

Crystal tells Crescenda that there are lots of opportunities in Atlanta. There's more money and no end to the drugs. So, they stash a little scratch away and move to Atlanta. Crescenda and Crystal try to work legitimate jobs for a month or so but then consider resorting to the only thing they know; they contemplate joining up with Ice Berg, a serious pimp who owns several high-rent blocks on the street.

AJ briefly heads back to the Hill's house. After about five months of marital disharmony, the couple is at each other's throats almost every day. More cursing and hurt come out of their mouths than anything else. Roy just tries to stay invisible, or he gets it from both ends.

No practice today (it's raining). Roy comes home a bit earlier than usual; he gets his chores done and completes homework before Margareta arrives around 4:30 p.m. They strike up a conversation (she's never really been interested in Roy's welfare before, but she is a bit more now as she's less interested in Bert). She asks about school and soccer, and she asks about Melody—Roy doesn't know anything. One of his classmates said he saw her downtown one night (Roy doesn't do anything about it now but intends to look for her on the streets, discreetly, later). Bert comes home, but first, Margareta tells Roy that they're planning a pizza night and will watch a movie together as a family. Roy is instantly pleased to be invited to join in, but reality quickly sets in, and he doesn't trust it. Bert comes home with a large family-size medium Maxi-Meat pizza and some inappropriate adult-themed movie. Margareta gets angry because "tonight was supposed to be for us, not just for you!" Margareta wanted a supreme pizza with veggies and a movie Roy could also watch; they started to argue, oblivious to Roy's presence. The argument escalates and devolves into sexual allegations. Roy silently retreats to his room, turns on the radio to drown out the noise, and prays.

Margareta and Bert start to throw objects. Bert breaks Margareta's mother's framed picture—Margareta reaches over to try to rescue it, but Bert perceives, intervenes, and quickly tears it up. Margareta slaps Bert, and Bert hits her back, sending her to the floor and giving her a bruise and cut on her cheek. Margareta hastily throws a few things in a suitcase with Bert yelling, "Go! I don't need you!" Bert hits the bottle as Margareta is leaving. He's so drunk about an hour after she's left that he passes out on the living room floor and doesn't make it to work the next day. Bert gives his manager some lame excuse, but he puts him on probation and is told, "One more unexcused absence or late, and you're fired!"

Part Five

Patton on Steroids

Chapter 36

After interactively reading books, sharing, and discussing interesting findings on the flora and fauna of Paradise, the group starts to have a discussion about what to do next. Karen feels a deep pang of guilt and overwhelming remorse. They ask her what's wrong, and she can't articulate it: "It's a terrible dread."

AJ reappears and instructs Karen to look deeply into his face. Just as in the previous experience, Karen is transported across dimensions and experiences what AJ observed (with a bit of thoughtful angelic editing).

"Roy!" Karen shouts as she stretches her arms to embrace him.

"Roy can't see you or hear you, Karen," AJ says gently. "Just enjoy your son's blessings and happiness." After a few moments of Karen's deep, breathless joy, AJ says, "Let's see Melody. Sorry, we can't see Melody at this time, Karen, I'm sorry."

"Why can't I see Melody? Is she alright? What's wrong, AJ?"

"I can't tell you; it won't do you or Melody any good. But she's not in imminent physical danger. But she's in grave spiritual danger."

"Please let me stay and help her, AJ. It won't be a problem, I won't be a problem; I'll obey whatever rules you set down, just let me help Melody. Please!" begs Karen.

"I won't pretend to fully understand or apprehend the pain and grief you're experiencing, but it's not my decision. God has established rules and boundaries. We must abide within those boundaries according to those rules," AJ says.

"God will be pleased if I help Melody return on the right path. The Scripture says that God wants everyone to be saved, doesn't it?" asks Karen.

"Yes, of course. But each person must make that decision for themselves. Melody is making her free will decisions. They're terrible decisions that will only harm her, but they're hers to make. Besides, I've tried to speak goodness and light to her, and she's not able to hear; voices of darkness are the only voices she hears," AJ says.

"She'll hear my voice!" Karen exclaims. "Remember the crippled man with four friends? Jesus forgave his sins based on the friends' faith, not the sinner's faith. So, that means God can and will save someone based on someone else's faith. God can use my faith to save Melody."

"You're correct, Karen. The Lord used the friends' faith to forgive the crippled man's sin rather than his own faith. Your request is highly irregular, but let's pray about this." The two pray in earnest. During the prayer, it's clear to both Karen and AJ that only Karen's faith is appropriate for application to Melody, but AJ should enjoin the prayers and tactical intercessions. It was also made known to them both that a Managing Angel would join them for their first intercessory attempt to bind the demon attempting to destroy Melody. The Managing Angel appears and introduces herself.

"Greetings, Karen, Jaynes. My name is Debriel. I'll be assisting you with your first intercession."

"We are honored, Angel Debriel," responds AJ.

"Melody is on a terrible path. She is fully capable of destroying herself without the help of a demon. But this demon, which is not fully formed yet, is an ugly one and will be a powerful adversary when fully developed. It presently doesn't have a name, but it will soon; its name will be Putrus. My job will be to establish a temporary boundary on Putrus's power so that his voice will be attenuated and your voices will be amplified. If Melody can't hear light over darkness, the cause is already lost. Your job will be to labor in intercession on behalf of Melody, speaking light and love to her, specifically, using your faith and love to speak Jesus into her soul."

"I think we understand," says AJ.

"Yes, we do. And thank you for this opportunity," adds Karen.

"My other job is to protect you both. As soon as I bind Putrus, Evil will bring the battle on two fronts; Melody's destruction will remain the first front, but you both will become the second front. Evil cannot reach or threaten you in Paradise but will seek to destroy you when you're out of Paradise's protection," Angel Debriel warns.

"I'm a little frightened," confesses Karen.

"Apprehension is appropriate. Do not underestimate the power of Evil or its commitment to destroying all in its path. Evil never sleeps; it never takes a vacation and is very deceptive. You can believe with conviction that you're doing good, doing God's will, when Evil is gleefully laughing because you're doing Evil's will. You must stay prayed-up to combat Evil and do battle in God's strength with God's methods and tools," responds Angel Debriel.

"What's the plan?" asks AJ.

"We'll all proceed together to intercept Melody. I'll intercept Purtrus and command him to remain within the boundary I establish. You will both begin your intercessory prayer and encouragement to Melody. I will remain with you until you have finished. We will then return to Paradise, and you may both engage in intercession once per solar cycle, that is, once a year, so time your intercessions wisely; this is the concession I'll grant for limiting Putrus's power. I'll pray the Name of the Lord over you so you may withstand the enemy's onslaught. Let's roll!" directs Angel Debriel.

The team travels to Melody, who's just finished a sexual encounter with Crystal. Angel Debriel intercepts what will soon become Putrus and commands his boundaries and limitations. The demon is hysterically enraged and prepares to leave and report what's just happened when it senses a conversation between Karen and AJ. "What is that? I've never seen a demon before. What an ugly, frightening, and utterly repulsive thing!" Karen says to AJ. In response, the demon transforms into a beautiful angel of light, turns toward Karen, smiles and winks, then disappears.

"Remember what Angel Debriel said: Evil can masquerade as good and light. That may be when perhaps it's most dangerous," advises AJ. "Now let's get to our intercession."

Karen and AJ begin intercession with prayer, pleading for mercy, grace, healing, deliverance, and salvation for Melody, with Angel Debriel looking on. They then transition to speaking encouragement directly to Melody. "I love you, God loves you, your name's Melody, not Crescenda, etc."

Melody does not appear to hear or react. Angel Debriel says, "This is going to be a marathon. It's not a sprint. Stay strong, keep the faith. You both did well. I bid you peace."

Karen and AJ return to Paradise.

Chapter 37

When Karen and AJ return, Karen's visibly shaken and trembling. Nora looks at AJ and motions; AJ doesn't respond, just looks concerned and focused on Karen. The group prays, and peace eventually overtakes Karen. She cannot recollect what's happened nor why she's so distraught. After shalom has displaced dread, she says she wants to head to Servan'ya. Claude reinforces Karen's undefined but obvious need right after her episode. "The Lord's going to do a work in Karen's life and in her loved ones' lives," Claude says.

The foursome exits the Library from the Balm of Gilead Gate on the South side of the Library. The Blessing Committee blesses each soul as they leave the Library. They can see a vast expanse of the Rapturous Meadow from the portico, sloping downward from the Library. Seemingly endless fields of dancing grasses and swaying wildflowers greet the troop as they proceed down the steps to their road south, the Highway of Goodness. At the edge of detectable vision to the South, the company can see what appears to be a dark, thick horizon, but it has no discernible form from this distance. They see small cities, towns, and villages scattered along the main roads and throughout the expansive fields interconnected by smaller roads. Nora spies a large flock of birds flying over the fields at a small distance and comments on their grace and synchronous movement—"like a single life form," says Nora.

The road leads to the Gallant Forest. The demarcation is abrupt between the expansive meadows surrounding the Library and the seemingly never-ending line of what appears to be a delightful mixture of various types of trees; the blurry, thick horizon is beyond the forest. The trees are enormous in comparison to earthly trees. Even though the company is still far off, it's apparent that this is a massive forest of redwood-sized trees. The day is ever-bright, though there's no sun (or moon or stars, for that matter), and nothing living in Paradise requires sleep, though some occasionally sleep to enjoy it as yet another gift from God.

There are a good deal more birds seen flying overhead, and a variety of brightly colored birds, some large, others small, are enjoyed. Occasionally, an animal traverses the road, going from one side of the meadow to the other. The animals don't seem to be frightened of the people, nor the other way around. The party encounters a tiger escorting a horse along a path. Karen inquires about the meaning of this scene from AJ, to which he replies, "There are no more predators and prey. In Paradise, there is peace, and there is no hunger and no need to replenish or refuel. Every living thing is returned to very near the perfect state in which God originally created them."

The conversation returns to the Archangel Michael, and Nora asks why she and Karen couldn't see Michael (though Nora could almost make out a silhouette). "He's so bright that few can, Nora. His brightness reflects God's glory, a by-product of standing directly in God's presence. All the Archangels have this same characteristic and effect on people and lower angels alike, just like when Moses had to veil his face from the people because his face shone brightly from being in God's presence," responds AJ.

"But Claude could see Michael, yet he's spiritually younger than me. I don't understand," remarks Karen.

"Claude appears young by choice; he's a spiritually mature soul, yet he refuses to grow up. God permits and is even delighted in Claude's childlike nature, so God is giving him the desire of his heart."

"So there!" Claude responds, sticking his tongue out at Nora. They have a nice laugh.

Karen asks AJ to describe Michael. "He has a huge masculine form, powerful, the personification of discipline. He wears a red tunic with a silver sash; two swords with highly polished blades of differing lengths and elaborately engraved hilts; an iron buckler about his waist; plain and simple war sandals; and a highly polished brass shield and helmet." The best way to define the Archangel Michael is that he's like "General Patton on steroids (times three billion)."

"I don't exactly know what that means, but I think I've got the picture," says Karen, asking, "When might I possibly be able to see Michael?"

AJ responds: "It's possible that it might not happen until the 'transformation,' but not likely given your rate of spiritual growth thus far. In fact, it seems as though you have a spiritual maturity index of about twenty-four. Our intercessory engagement must have matured you significantly and taken its toll."

"What intercessory engagement?" Karen asks.

"I'm not at liberty to speak openly about it. But that was why you were so upset when you returned to Paradise. You were involved in a mission of supreme importance, which you and only you can undertake."

"What mission, AJ?" Nora asks. "Please tell us."

"Perhaps in the future, not now. Peace," AJ replies. "What was your question about Michael, Karen?"

"If I can't stand before Michael, how can I stand before God?" Karen asks.

"Good question, Karen. You can't. No one can, not even the Archangel Michael, if it weren't for God's love and mercy. We will all stand before God based on His love and mercy, never based on our own merit, not man nor angel."

AJ excuses himself and says he has an earthly errand he must return to. He detours to briefly visit with Angel Sarai.

Chapter 38

"Hello, Sarai. Greetings and peace to you in the Name of our Lord."

"Greetings, Jaynes. It's so good to see you. How goes the battle with human combatants?"

"It's challenging, my friend. The loved ones of my Karen are mostly making terrible choices to continue and delve deeper into sin and closer to destruction. When Karen asks for their status, it breaks her heart each time she witnesses their state. I'm so angry with Melody and Bert for throwing their lives away and throwing away the gift of God that I could chew nails! Bert's demon, Poison, is accelerating Bert's demise. Melody has a demon forming and only listens to darkness; she comprehensively rejects the light," AJ expounds.

"Interesting, tell me more."

"Roy's doing well and was recently adopted into God's Family."

"I know, I heard; I'm so happy for him and you, Jaynes."

"Yes, thank God for Roy. He makes Karen's heart glad."

"You seem to have really grown into a sympathetic engagement with your case. How is that possible? I thought you didn't like humans."

"Who said I didn't like humans? Now, don't go putting words into my mouth. I've always loved people. Some of my best friends are people."

"Blah, blah, blah," Sarai quips with a smile.

"Of course, you're right, and you were right. I couldn't see it. But now I'm beginning to feel God's love for His human creation. Love is based on empathy, out of their pain, and a longing for redemption and restoration."

"It takes a big angel to admit when he's mistaken. Bravo, Jaynes."

"Nonsense. I've admitted you've been wrong many times, Sarai."

They both enjoy the fellowship of a good laugh.

"A dramatic and disruptive change has been requested and permitted. Karen requested that she be allowed to add her faith to Melody's. The Lord has allowed Karen to intercede in prayer and encourage Melody. We just completed the first intercession and may continue to do so once a year. Melody, of course, had a demon trying to accelerate her death. The observation of a demon was a traumatic shock to Karen; she may have some PTSD, and she's at risk every time she leaves Paradise to conduct an intercession for Melody."

"You carry a significant burden, my brother; I'll continue to pray for you and your Karen," says Sarai.

AJ takes his leave and continues to Earth.

Roy's estrangement at home intensifies, yet he persists in attending church. As he walks to church one cool morning (the couple that offered to drive Roy to church became variable and unreliable after several months, so Roy walks now), he questions God as he prays, "Why is my life worse now than before? Why doesn't anyone like me?" AJ tries to comfort him, but Roy's too angry to listen. "Why did You have to take my mom? Why didn't You take my dad?" Roy continues.

AJ warns Roy, "God knows you're hurting, Roy, but you must stop feeling sorry for yourself. That only invites evil. Remember the good people God has brought into your life, Coach Binder …"

As Roy struggles, a shadow begins to develop, takes notice, and starts trying to whisper to him, "God is so unfair. What did I ever do to deserve this? Why—"

"Be gone!" AJ commands.

"He's invited me," the evil spirit responds.

"He did not invite you. He belongs to the Light and the Truth! Be gone!" AJ continues. "Roy, your sister needs your prayers; pray for her. Your dad needs your prayers. Pray for him. They don't have a Coach in their lives. Kindle your compassion, Roy …"

Roy's heart softens, and the shadow dissipates as he begins to pray for Melody.

***

"What's that smell?" Barry asks later that week at school as Roy walks past to the adjacent lunch table. "It's you! Ah man, you stink twerp! Get outta here!"

Roy didn't have any clean shirts, so he wore this one just a day longer than he should have. Not only does it smell, but it's visibly dirty. Roy's very embarrassed at Barry's loud insult, but he's more ashamed of his lack. Somehow, when you're in middle school, if you lack, you feel it's a personal reflection of your unworthiness. Roy sits down without making eye contact with the three other kids at the table. Some kids in the lunchroom have trays of hot food; others bring a lunch. Roy brings a lunch bag with an onion and wadded-up paper in a baggy to give the appearance that he has lunch. He opens the bag and ruffles through its contents, pretending not to be hungry or interested in food. Roy's well-rehearsed at trying not to bring attention to himself, but his brown paper bag has been used a few times and is weak; it breaks, spilling the contents of his pretend lunch on the table, the onion falling and rolling down the floor.

"What's that, you weirdo?" says one of the boys at the table. "Barry, look what your friend's having for lunch!"

The kid grabs the paper stuffed in a baggy and throws it to Barry, who opens it and searches for something edible wrapped in the paper.

"Paper? You eat paper? I wanna see you eat this paper, twerp!" Barry blasts as he and his buds walk over to Roy.

"Leave Roy alone, or I'm telling!" Becca warns Barry as she stands between him and Roy.

Stunned at being challenged by a girl, Barry nervously scoffs and returns to his lunch. Becca picks up the onion and hands it to Roy, sitting there with his head down.

"He can be such a jerk," Becca says.

"I don't need a girl to—" says Roy.

"I can't eat all my lunch. My mom always packs too much," says Becca.

"That's okay. No thanks," responds Roy.

"Please, take my apple sauce and carrots. They'll just go to waste," Becca says as she hands them to Roy.

"Thanks," Roy responds softly, lifting his eyes briefly to make contact and darting away as Becca motions for her girlfriends to come over and join them.

"My friends call me B-dog or Rebee," she offers.

"I'll just call you Becca. It's pretty," Roy says.

Kids in Roy's class, even the teachers, started quietly bringing an item to share with Roy during lunch. Though they tried hard not to embarrass Roy, he understood that they understood. AJ commends the folks who do this.

***

One day, Mr. Isaacs, this month's lunch monitor, feigned being paged to an urgent situation right after he bought a hot lunch, which he thanked Roy for accepting as he ran off to solve the imaginary circumstance.

"Lord, please bless this humble man and his house," AJ prays. "Please minister to these young souls who have ministered to Roy;

some tenderly, others clumsily but sincerely. And thank You for showing Roy that he's valued."

Roy and Becca make a date to go to the library after school one day.

"What kinda book are you looking for?" Roy asks Becca.

"I need a book on Roman Caesars for my report. But I'd also like to find a novel, just for fun. What about you?"

"There's this great book I heard about on the internet. It's about a guy that becomes a hero when he battles an entire army of—"

"That sounds like a boys' book, Roy. Don't waste your breath," says Becca.

"Yeah, sorry. I'm gonna see if I can find something good," Roy says.

"Let's meet back at the librarian's desk in thirty minutes," Becca suggests.

"Thirty? I only need five at the most," says Roy.

"Well, I'll need thirty. So—"

Roy finds a great boys' book with lots of pictures and action, sits down at a study table, and starts to read while waiting for his friend. Becca plops a couple of books on the table and pulls up a chair beside Roy.

"What ya reading?" Becca asks as she reads the title.

"It's a boys' book," responds Roy, "but it's good so far; I'm about halfway through it."

"I've got some news," Becca says. Roy stops reading, lifts his head, and makes eye contact.

"My dad's got a new job. And we're moving to Chicago," Becca reports.

"When?" asks Roy.

"Around the beginning of summer. I'm not sure exactly when," she responds sadly.

"Are you glad?" Roy asks.

"Kinda. I guess. My dad says it'll be good for the family, but I hate to leave all my friends."

"Well, we can stay friends by writing and stuff," advises Roy.

"Yeah, but it's not the same," Becca confesses.

"You'll make new friends. It's easy for you," Roy comments.

"You'll make new friends too," Becca tries to reassure Roy.

"You were the first kid to be nice to me. After that day in the lunchroom, other kids also started to be nice to me. Thanks for being my friend," Roy says.

"You don't thank someone for being a friend, silly," Becca instructs.

"You didn't have to, but you did and made school good again. Thanks, I'll miss you. Good luck in Chicago," Roy says.

"It'll be okay, Roy. Be happy for her, for all your friends as they graduate from one circumstance to another," AJ says. "This is an important life lesson." AJ then leaves to see Melody.

***

Crystal walks up to Crescenda at the appointed venue after searching in vain for several hours for a fix—neither woman succeeded. It's a dark corner lit by flickering neon. AJ sees a demon agitating both women. "I was better off in Little Hope! Why did I hav'ta listen to dis tart?"

"You said Atlanta was full of scratch hussy! I ain't had nothin' in days!" Crescenda shouts. "I've been trying to make it legit for a month, and noth'n!"

"Chill floozy. I got this lead," Crystal says.

"What kinda lead? I know what kinda leads you get. I don't wanna hear about it."

"You wanna get high?" Crystal asks. "Okay, then shut up and listen. You remember we talked about hooking up with Ice Berg; he owns half the east side. His madams say he's good to 'em. We can start tonight, and he'll give us a free taste before we hit the streets."

The demon encourages Crescenda, "I just need a little, just to get me by. It's been too long. I don't hav'ta hustle for long, jus 'til some'n turns up…"

AJ tries to speak to Crescenda. "Melody, this is not who you are. Your mother didn't raise you for this…"

"Save your breath, angel, she's ours!" The demon laughs.

"Okay, okay. Where do we find this son-of-a-streetwalker?" asks Crescenda.

So Crescenda and Crystal hook up with Ice Berg in Atlanta. The pimp has been in the biz for over six years since his last release. He has a lot of cash, connections, and several streetwalkers. Ice Berg wasn't particular. Any girl was a potential moneymaker. She didn't have to be too young or pretty; she just had to hustle and give him his cut. So, he was cool when Crescenda and Crystal introduced themselves as C&C, showing up needing a fix, protection, and a gig. Crescenda began her formal career of prostitution under the expert tutelage of Ice Berg (she considered the trix she played under Tough Nuts weren't 'professional').

About 1 a.m. Ice Berg makes his rounds. C&C both have turned a trick and have some cash for Ice Berg, who is pleased and invites them to crash at his crib. "I protect my tarts. I be good to 'em, too, if they be good to me," Ice Berg states.

The crib is a two-bedroom apartment on the third floor. Ice Berg has two such apartments in this building; one's for his streetwalkers to crash and burn, and the other is for business. Ice Berg himself lives in another part of town, in a building he owns. The women use the crib to crash, eat crap, and get high. This is the extent of the ambition of almost all his women. However, Crescenda is still naive enough to dream of a better life with a man who really cares for her—she is going to get off the streets soon, but in the meantime, there's time for one more high.

While at the crib, reveling in a meth high that first night, Crescenda makes the mistake of saying out loud that she's gonna get off the streets.

"Yeah? Sure, we all gonna get off the streets," one of the women says and laughs.

"And get married," another scoffs.

The demon, sensing a ripe moment to escalate tensions, further agitated the women: "She thinks she's better 'n us! She thinks she's too good to work! Heck, she ain't even that pretty!"

"You think you're too good to work, tramp?" one of the girls demands. "Com'n 'roun here with your suburban crap! I'll give you some learning in street-life hussy!"

The women begin to fight. Ice Berg laughs; he likes his streetwalkers to have some spunk. His only interest is in protecting his investment. "Jus' don't damage the face!"

AJ leaves, disgusted with Melody's choices and situation and reluctantly heads off to see how Bert's making out.

Bert wasted no time hitting the bar scene (since Margareta moved out). He started dating right away. Several women were hanging around the bars, ridden-hard women, street-wise women, "I know what I want, and I don't want a permanent relationship" women. These women were good for a few laughs and a couple one-night stands, a few of them. The more unhealthy ones might cling desperately, but most had learned that game only drives 'em away faster. Bert was drinking heavily, draining his finances, and Roy was left with the responsibility of trying to keep up the place inside and out to some minimum level of decency.

Margareta wastes no time in retaining an attorney and slapping Bert with divorce papers, alleging mental and emotional cruelty and suffering, and demanding half interest in Bert's house, furniture, and all tangible assets, including his retirement account. Bert retains an attorney who reinforces that even though the marriage was short, it'll be tough to fight it, and fighting it may cost almost as much as the settlement. This drives Bert over the edge, much to Poison's, Bert's personal demon's, delight. Bert starts buying drugs on short-term credit at his favorite bars. When he doesn't pay up, he gets beaten up and threatened, resulting in the bartenders throwing him out and petty dealers looking for him.

Bert meets several women, and the relationship generally lasts one to two dates. Bert is pretty pessimistic about women and the whole marriage thing, on the one hand, but he is simultaneously too needy to renounce them completely due to his instinctively knowing that he was drowning. At work, Bert's coworkers are complaining to his manager—*he's not getting his work done, and it's making us all look bad*. His manager first counsels him and then gives him a stern reprimand.

"How dare he condescend to me. What gives him the right to judge me?" Poison spews. "He'd just crawl under a rock and die if he went through the pain I'm go'n through. What a lousy manager!"

"Look, I've had a tough time recently, but I'm the best professional in the office. I can run circles around these fools. Heck, I've saved this company," Bert retorts.

"What are you talking about, Bert? Saved this company?" his manager asks. "Look, take the rest of the day off and get some rest. Come back refreshed tomorrow, and we'll talk again."

"You think about it and get some rest! We will talk about it tomorrow, and maybe I'll go over your head, and we'll see just who's the most valuable to this company!" Bert exclaims as he stomps out of his manager's office.

"That's show'n 'em, boy! He'll be sorry when I go to the director; he'll be begg'n me to stay! I'll demand a raise and promotion …" Poison says to Bert.

Chapter 39

AJ returns to Paradise and catches up with the trio still in the Rapturous Meadows.

"Friends, coming down the road up ahead, are two servants of God. A word of warning: these two men are the only people of flesh in Paradise. God has chosen them for an extraordinary mission back on Earth. Don't defocus them. They're preparing and have been preparing for this mission for thousands of Earth years. And you thought Beethoven was belaboring for a long time!" says AJ.

"Welcome back, friend. Who are they?" asks Karen.

"Elijah and Enoch. They're traveling to the Library to join the high council meeting," AJ responds.

"I remember. Elijah is a prophet, and Enoch was the one whom God took before he died," Nora adds.

"Yes, that's right. They are the only two human beings taken by God before death to reside in Paradise. God did this to prepare them for their mission, which will be as witnesses to the people of Israel during the first half of the time of Jacob's Troubles. They will witness the love, salvation, faithfulness, and goodness of God to Jacob, and they will witness against the sins of Israel, but Israel won't believe them. They will kill them, but it is their great undying honor to serve as the final testament of God to the people of Israel before the final judgment," AJ concludes.

"A profound responsibility indeed," Karen says.

"I will address Angel Hess, their angel, who never leaves their presence, and see if they are willing to step aside and meet with you for a few moments," AJ says, then briefly communes with Angel Hess while they are still far away. "Yes, they will step aside and make your acquaintance. When you meet them, give a respectful greeting and remember these are very passionate men of God on a mighty mission. They are not to be taken lightly. They won't speak to you directly but will communicate through Angel Hess."

A couple of moments later, they see Enoch and Elijah walking together with a small group, a couple of people in front and a few behind. Enoch's and Elijah's white robes are different from other robes. They are rougher and not as bright. The men are very old in appearance with long flowing white hair and beards. Their continence seems veiled or dull compared to others they have met; they still carry the burdens of life and sins in their bodies, the obligations of the people.

"Behold, the chosen of the Lord, do favor us. Blessed be the Name of the Lord," AJ greets the group.

"Amen. God's faithful witnesses, Enoch and Elijah, greet the Lord's sisters and brothers. The Lord's favor upon you and yours forever, amen," responds Angel Hess. "How may we serve you?"

"Sirs, we just have a couple of questions, please. What was life like when you walked the Earth?" asks Nora.

"The glory of God was evident everywhere, in the beauty and practical goodness of the world He created, in the sunrise and sunset, in the lakes, rivers, fields, meadows, mountains, stars, in the flowers of the field, and in the animals He created. Yet man's inhumanity to man, sin, and wickedness stained the world. Man's fallen nature corrupted goodness and beauty and compromised creation. Man's sinful nature cast a long shadow on life, and death entered. Death to man, death to every living thing, and most importantly, death in God's and man's relationship," responds Angel Hess on behalf of Enoch.

"I remember great wickedness growing unchecked. The people of God, aware of His existence but not truly knowing Him, turned away from the living God to worship false idols. These idols were crafted from various materials, including stone, wood, and metal. People believed that if they covered all the bases, their lives with their neighbors would be better on Earth, and they'd be assured of a life in Heaven, somebody's Heaven, anybody's Heaven. People believed that all they had to do was worship the one right god out of the many, and that would be their fire insurance. The problem with that philosophy is that false gods don't care if other false gods are worshipped or not. But the living God does care. He's a jealous God and will not tolerate His people worshipping other gods. His people must be faithful to Him, and this is where the people consistently failed. We were like a harlot running from man to man. Yet God forgave us, again and again, and we returned to sin, again and again," responds Angel Hess on behalf of Elijah.

"Why did God choose you?" asks Karen.

"That's a great mystery; I am so unworthy," answers Angel Hess for the men, but then adds his own editorial, "These men love God and are very close to Him; God trusts these men."

"What's your mission?" asks Karen.

"We are to be witnesses to Israel, and the nations, during the first part of the Last Days; witnesses of the goodness and salvation of God and against the Beast and enemy of God and man."

"Have you seen God?" asks Nora.

"We have not seen God, but we commune with Him in Spirit. We know and do His will."

"What is God like?" asks Nora.

"Only God is God. God is holiness, purity, goodness, salvation, justice, and love. Man cannot comprehend God, and to the degree we commune with God, we may do this only by His love and grace. Be advised that Michael and the other Archangels and Seraphim feel the same way in God's presence as you felt in Michael's presence. God is absolute perfection, and only the most faithful love and sincere fearfulness is appropriate as our human and angelic response before Him," Angel Hess remarks.

"Thank you, brothers, for taking time with us. May the Lord bless His mission and ministry through you, and may you bring Him much good fruit. Amen," says Nora.

"May the Lord continue to make you into the image of His Son, and may you rest well in our Lord's Sabbath. Amen," responds Angel Hess on behalf of Enoch and Elijah, and they take their leave.

After some traveling along the road, they enter the enormous woods, Gallant Forest, which spans the base of a mountain range called the Redemption Range. The road itself is a well-packed dirt road that changes in hue slightly from a deep brown to a dark tan once inside the boundary of the forest. Occasional trees tower above the heads of the travelers, so much so that they can scarcely make out the treetops. The coniferous trees have very dark green needles of various types. There are a variety of deciduous type trees, each having a whole crop of leaves of different shades of greens, reds, yellows, oranges, and browns, and in various sizes. Some trees have very rough bark, and others are smoother; there are even birch-type trees with their beautiful peeling white bark. The leaves of the deciduous trees change color from green to orange to brown, etc., from time to time so that a rolling kaleidoscope of colors moves through the forest's canopy like an organic lifeform. This living canopy is well above the heads of the trio, as in the Amazon. The volume of space seems to make its own microclimate conducive to living things of a great variety.

Several small groups of people pass the troupe as those groups venture on toward the Library. Members of the groups politely greet the trio in passing and continue. Thus far, no group or individual traveling in the same direction as the group has overtaken the troupe; apparently, no one is in a hurry here in Paradise. The road in the forest is winding, so they would have little preparation before encountering a group traveling in the other direction. Just as in the meadowlands, many animals can be seen either crossing the road or not too far into the woods.

"There's so much mental reflection and silence here in Paradise. I think I'll ask the next group we come across what they're discussing or feeling," states Karen.

"Well, you won't have to wait long, my dear," responds Nora.

Just then, two gentlemen are seen walking toward the trio, deep in discussion.

"Greetings, brothers. I am Karen, and this is Nora, Claude, and Angel Jaynes. May God grant you peace and multiply your pleasures," says Karen in greeting.

"Hello, sisters Karen and Nora, and brothers Claude and Angel Jaynes. May the good God likewise bless you with His continued benevolence. My friend here is Michael, and I am John. What may we do for you?" answers John, the taller of the two men; both appear to be approximately the same age.

"You seemed so intent in your discussion; I was just wondering what the topic was. Please pardon my curiosity if it's too personal."

"Not at all, Karen. We were discussing some finer points of theology. You see, my friend here is quite a scholar, and I wanted to benefit from his knowledge and wisdom."

"You're too kind, John. It is you who are the scholar. Our theological topic is on God's *election* of the saints. We were reviewing scriptures and had previously asked God to open our understanding," answers Michael.

"What does the election refer to?" asks Karen.

"It's a doctrine put forward by several of the writers of the Old Testament and the Lord's disciple Peter and his apostle Paul, and later advanced significantly by Reformists in the Middle Ages. It refers to God's election, or selection, of those individuals who would belong to Him from before God's creation of the Earth. That is, those that would be pre-selected to be *saved*," Michael says.

"I thought that everyone was given the opportunity to be saved?" Karen says.

"Everyone is. And yet God has pre-determined those who will be saved. Both conditions are simultaneously true. It is this difficulty that we were discussing," answers John.

"Has God given you the answer?" asks Nora.

"God has given us each other, and we pray and discuss and pray again. God so blesses me to have my friend, Michael, with whom I can discuss this burning question," responds John.

"Likewise, the pleasure and satisfaction of John's companionship has all but eclipsed the question. I should almost hate to have the answer, as that might redirect or change our friendship from this living thing that it is," says Michael.

"Your friendship is a beautiful thing. May you both prosper and magnify the Lord in it," says Karen, and they take their leave.

"Karen, Nora. I don't know if you know of these men, but the taller one, John, is John Calvin, the great theologian. The other is Michael Serventus, a physician and amateur scholar. John and Michael knew each other on Earth but were enemies. In fact, John was instrumental in condemning Michael to death as a heretic. As a part of their individual healing and maturation, God made them the best of friends over the very topic that caused them to be enemies on Earth. God is so good," remarks AJ.

"Amen!" is the response from the companions.

"So, God made two bitter enemies the best of friends. If I remember correctly, Michael was burned at the stake. Yet, now they are inseparable. Only God could do this. He really does want His children to love one another. It's such a beautiful picture. I'll think I'll paint it!" Claude exclaims.

"How do you paint God's love, Claude? Even as the world's greatest artist, how can it be done?" asks Nora.

"It's easy, my sister. God's already done it many times. It's the story of His Son, the story of Michael and John, and every person's story when they forgive another. I just need to copy His work," Claude explains.

"You artists have extraordinary insight; you must represent the best of humanity," Karen says.

"Well, perhaps French artists anyway," Claude teases.

AJ pardons himself for another trip to Earth. He'll start with Roy.

Chapter 40

"Roy." Coach motions for him to come quickly over. "I've got an idea. You've become quite a faithful young man. Even though we've only got a few games left, I'd like you to be the team chaplain. Whittaya think, son?"

"We'll have six games if we make it to the playoffs, Coach," responds Roy.

"Now that's faith!" retorts Coach.

"You don't think we can make the playoffs, Coach?" asks Roy. "What does a team chaplain do?"

"The team chaplain is the players' go-to guy for spiritual and emotional issues. Guys might say somethin' like, 'I get mad at my kid brother for breaking my stuff. I know I should pray for him, but I'm too mad. What should I do?' What would you say to him, Roy?"

"Wow, that's a hard problem, Coach. I'd say he needs to pray for his brother, and as he does, God will change his heart, and pretty soon, he won't be mad anymore," Roy responds. "Is that right?"

"That's exactly right. Good job. You're the team chaplain; I'll make an announcement now."

"Way to go, Roy! I'm proud of you," AJ says in a sort of spiritual high-five.

Barry and his buds find out and persecute him three times; when Roy doesn't respond as desired, they lose interest. But when Roy sees them picking on another kid, he steps in to protect and the boys back down. Becca is impressed by Roy's compassion and integrity.

***

After completing homework one day, Roy turns the radio on to his Christian station, and someone is asking whether the listener has anyone in spiritual danger. He immediately thinks of his dad and Melody and starts to pray, "God, please help my dad and my sister, Melody. I don't even know where she is, but I'm worried she's not taking good care of herself. Mom loved her and always tried to take good care of my sister; please step in and care for Melody. I don't know what's wrong with Dad, but something's very wrong. Please forgive him for being mean and help him. I don't know how to help him, Lord, or even how to pray for him, Sir."

"Very nice, Roy," AJ says. "Ask God to show you how to pray for your family. Ask God to draw them unto Himself, to save, redeem, and restore each. Ask God to rebuke evil from each of them and open their eyes and hearts to His love and beauty."

Roy continues in prayer, "And God, please let my sister and my dad know that I love them and that You love them too. And please make Melody call me or write me a letter or something, so I know she's all right. Thank you."

A short time later, Bert comes home and heads for the bottle, then for the bedroom to prepare for another night on the town. He doesn't greet Roy, make his supper, or inquire about how Roy may be doing. After Bert leaves without a word to Roy, Roy rummages through the icebox and cabinets to scrounge something to eat. Roy finds some stale saltines and a can of soup. Before he eats, he prays for his dad, "Dear God, my dad's so hurt he doesn't even know what he's doing. Please don't be too angry with him. Forgive him and help him to get better so we can be a family again."

"My dear Roy, be at peace. Your father's in other hands now. There's nothing more you can do for him. Focus on being faithful to God and abiding with Him in peace," AJ offers. "Lord Almighty, please spare this precious soul more grief and pain. Protect him from his biological father's demise. Keep him from the gravity of the sinful eddy currents Bert develops as he self-destructs. Shield him from the sins of his biological father, please. Amen."

AJ heads off to see Melody.

Crescenda wanted to get her own flat, since she was constantly abused by the other girls at Ice Berg's crib. But she had no money, of course. Crystal wasn't too interested in moving from the crib, but a woman named Pixie was interested. The two women planned to save some money, get an apartment, and find jobs—they would get off the streets before it was too late and no longer dreamed of anything but the streets. The demon, Putrus, was more substantial in form now. Putrus was very aggravated and threatened both of them: "You losers will never make it! You can't get off the streets. There are no jobs for trash like you! You're druggies, always will be …"

But AJ perceived a narrow window of opportunity and spoke encouragement to the women. "You can do this! You can get a job and clean up. You can get off the streets! Get off the streets! Do it now …" The women were listening. The demon was growing slightly weaker.

Unfortunately, even though they had saved a few hundred dollars, you can't get an apartment without a job, or a job without an apartment, so they languish. The demon, sensing his own opportunity, accused God, and the women became more angry and agitated.

In a last-ditch effort, AJ convinced Pixie they must get out now by heading to the Dorothy Day House. Pixie convinced Crescenda, and the two headed to the shelter the next day—neither was used to venturing out in the daylight. Unfortunately, the shelter was full, but it was suggested that the women try the Salvation Army.

"No way in heck I'm go'n to the Salvation Army!" Crescenda exclaims. "All they do is preach at you!"

"It's our only option, Crescenda. You want to get off the streets. Okay then, let's do this together," Pixie exhorts.

AJ and Pixie both continue to encourage Melody, and she eventually concedes. The women head for the Salvation Army later in the afternoon—they know they must get in line early if they want a bed. They're given a healthy dinner and beds for the night. There is a compulsory Bible study and prayer service, of course. Pixie is moved and responds to the invitation for God's forgiveness. Another angel materializes and accompanies Pixie, whose real name is Lisa White. The demon is now free to focus on Crescenda. Crescenda becomes more furious with God as she unconsciously realizes that she is alone again since Lisa will be traveling another path.

AJ leaves to find Bert.

Bert met Sylvia at a bar, of course. Sylvia was previously married once. She had been divorced for about ten years, seeing several men, typically for a year or two, before ending the relationship. Bert and Sylvia started dating and became serious (three dates). However, Bert was pretending to be financially secure (which was rare in her previous encounters) and lavished her with gifts, flowers, dinner out, jewelry, and pornographic movies rather than paying the mortgage payments. Poison is encouraging the relationship.

The mortgage bank is now calling every day, at home and the office. The voice-mail is full and can't accept any more messages from bill collectors (Sylvia says it's all the women after hot Bert, which Bert doesn't mind, though he's in too much distress to let it go to his head for more than a few seconds). Bill collectors have been calling Bert at work, and Bert's growing ever more hostile; he's yelling at the bill collectors and refusing to answer his phone. The whole office is in turmoil due to Bert's agitation and anger. Poison leverages this devolving circumstance to drive Bert rapidly toward a psychotic break—he starts seeing bugs everywhere, first crawling on things, then crawling on him, in his food, and swimming in the water as he showers. Bert rationalizes that he needs to marry Sylvia quickly to provide some grounding and stability to his compromised reality.

Up until this time, Bert's always gone over to Sylvia's. Bert made excuses for not wanting to bring her home to his house (it seems Bert forgot to mention to Sylvia that he has a son and daughter). But Bert breaks down and brings her home one evening. They come home with Chinese and a pornographic movie, talking dirty and acting smutty as they walk in the door. Roy's in Bert's chair watching reruns on TV when the door bursts open with laughter and cursing in drunken anticipation. Roy panics, jumps out of the chair, and immediately begins to apologize; he stops when he sees Sylvia. Sylvia likewise shuts up as soon as she sees Roy and, in a state of shock, turns to Bert and demands, "What the heck is this? Do you think I'm some dumb vixen? You never said noth'n 'bout having no kids! Screw you, Bert!" Poison's screaming at both of them, fomenting psychotic rage in them both.

Roy escapes and hides in his bedroom while they're preoccupied with yelling at each other—Poison tries to get them to notice Roy and direct their rage toward him, but AJ makes a solemn command from God, and Poison shrinks back and refocuses on Bert and Sylvia. Bert's drinking before Sylvia's out the door, and he's so incensed that he forgets about Roy and gets back into his car and heads off to a bar, any bar. He's not welcome in any bars close to his home.

When Bert returns after the bar closes, he remembers Roy and goes into his room yelling, falling, and making no rational sense. He hits Roy a couple of times. Roy manages to use the pillow as protection, and then Bert falls again, barfs on the floor, hitting Roy's blanket with stinking puke, and crawls out of the bedroom only to pass out in the hallway.

Roy cries and prays—his room stinks of partially digested alcohol and barf. Roy cleans himself and his room up and cries to sleep. AJ intercedes on Roy's behalf. "Lord, thank you for intervening and protecting from the full extent of intended harm. Please shield him further, Sir. This innocent soul is being violated in so many dimensions; I beseech you, God, to take steps on Roy's behalf …"

Poison is outside Roy's room laughing. He knows the steps God may take to protect Roy might involve the acceleration of Bert's damnation.

AJ returns to Paradise via Angel Sarai.

Chapter 41

"This isn't going to work, Sarai," AJ says with desperation. "I just can't stand some people. I have no patience or tolerance for them. They destroy themselves and with themselves, the gift of life that God has given them and the gift of His image in them. And if that wasn't bad enough, they bring others down. I just hate some of them. I'm sorry, but I do," vents AJ.

"Shalom, my brother, be at peace," counsels Sarai.

"How can I be at peace under these tragic circumstances, sister?"

"What has transpired, my brother?" Sarai asks calmly.

"Melody's a tragic and pathetic case. She's destroying herself in sin; she won't listen to the truth or come into the light. Bert is so bent on damnation that he's not even in the pathetic range any longer. I don't know what else to do, Sarai. I want off this case."

"As grievous as the situation is, AJ, it's simpler than you're perceiving," Sarai says. "You're hating the sin, which is right. But you're confounding the sin and the sinner, which is wrong. Remember, God hates sin, but He loves the sinner. Remember that while you hate the sin and its consequence, God, and you, still love the sinner."

"That's just it, Sarai. I'm not sure I do love some of them," AJ maligns.

"Trust me, AJ, you do. It's simply not in you to hate what God loves. I know this to be true. I will pray for you," Sarai says. "Dear Father, please restore my dear brother back into uncompromised fellowship with You and his charge. His zeal for Your honor has blinded him to the truth of Your limitless forgiveness and forbearance, especially toward those that deserve it least. Grant him rest and bid him peace as he continues to perform according to Your will. Amen."

Angel Sarai receives a revelation. "Brother, your crisis is not organic or happenstance. Evil has done this to you. You're being attacked as soon as you travel to Earth. You must keep in prayer. These attacks won't stop. You're a marked target since you and Karen intervened to intercede for Melody. Be careful of Karen if you allow her to accompany you to Earth again. If Evil's impact on you is so powerful, multiply it by a thousand for Karen; it may destroy her," Angel Sarai warns.

AJ and AS are empathetic siblings, but both are seriously alarmed at new developments. AJ meets up with the trio.

AJ's countenance appears downcast to the company, and they solicit the whys and wherefores. AJ only shares that "the human condition is so desperate that sometimes even angels despair." So, the company takes a moment to stop and intercede for AJ with God.

"Dear Heavenly Father, we perceive that some human situation has burdened our friend, and we ask that You minister Your love, strength, and encouragement to him. Strengthen him and give him peace," Nora prays.

"Perfect Prince of Peace, please touch AJ with Your healing power. Please don't allow anyone or anything to steal his joy! Amen," Karen prays.

AJ is visibly touched by the prayers on his behalf, particularly Karen's since her loved ones have burdened him.

"High King of Heaven, arrayed in living light, enlighten our brother's path again and minister peace unto him even as he bears unbearable burdens. Lighten his load, please. Amen," Claude prays.

"AJ, do you weep?" Nora asks.

"I have never been so overcome with love, my friends. I'm in awe that you have ministered to me thus. I now see and have experienced the Master's own living love, not from the Majesty, but from His image in human beings. I'm beginning to understand why God loves humankind," AJ confesses.

"Once you do understand, please explain it to me 'cause I'm lost on that one," Karen says, half laughing. "A song just popped into my head," she continues. "Born Free, as the wind's free …" Karen sings. "Oh no, I think I messed that up pretty good," she says, laughing. "I don't understand it, but someone needs to hear this song to lift their spirit." The music and lyrics are in everyone's head, and all join in for several errant choruses.

The fellowship continues along the road. They smell wonderful scents of fresh pine and varieties of fruit blossoms, and even though the trees are so tall they could block the sun, there are no shadows cast, no darkness anywhere.

Deep into the heart of the forest along the road, the companions (AJ had just taken his leave) encounter a senior-looking woman walking toward the direction of the Library. She has a beautiful white robe, unlike any other observed thus far. She's wearing a garland on her head, a gold sash draped across her upper body, and white sandals. There are many people in her entourage, following her on all sides. As the groups approach each other, Nora greets the senior Lady.

"Hello, favored sister. May you enjoy the Lord's eternal presence in your life forevermore. I am Nora, and these are my friends, Karen and Claude. We are but humble servants of the Most High at your service and your company's service."

"Hello, sisters. I am Irena Sendler, the most favored of our Lord's lowest servants. My companions are faithful friends who walked with me on Earth. How may I help you?"

"Your countenance is striking. We just wanted to meet you and hear your story."

"My story is not worth hearing, my child, but God's story through me is. God gave me the privilege of rescuing Jews in Poland during the Nazi occupation; some of them are in my company. I used my position as a nurse to smuggle Jewish children out of the ghetto before the Nazis could kill or transfer them to the camps. I was so grateful to God for allowing me the privilege to save Jews. God is good, Amen."

"Amen," responds the company.

"Irena, you say that there are Jews in your company of friends. I don't understand. I thought only Christians were going to be saved," comments Karen.

"I recall from my life on Earth one day that someone asked me, 'Do Jews have to become Christians to be saved?' I thought about it and recalled that Christianity is an offshoot of Judaism. Paul teaches us in the Book of Romans that the Jews are the natural branch that was broken off the olive tree, and Gentile Christians are the wild olive branch that was grafted in. He then further teaches us that the Jews will be grafted back into the tree and that 'salvation is of and for the Jew first and also the Gentile.' So, you see, Karen, it's not the Jews that are foreigners to Paradise, but we Gentiles. And concerning these Jews, they know and love Jesus our Messiah," Irena says.

"I see. I think I understand. But what about Muslims, Hindus, Buddhists, and even Pagans? Certainly, they won't be saved. They don't believe in Jesus," comments Karen.

"Abraham's true descendants are God's chosen people, and we Christians are allowed to worship God and abide in God as Abraham's spiritual descendants. Abraham's spiritual descendants can theoretically include Muslims, Hindus, Buddhists, and even Pagans. Being a spiritual descendant of Abraham is based on a heart attitude toward God. It's about relationships, not religion. All those who love and obey God, even Pagans, can obey God's law in their hearts if they're Abraham's spiritual descendants. God knows all people who love Him, and He hasn't and will never lose a single soul that belongs to Him. Many souls that belong to God love and obey Jesus without knowing His name, understanding His atoning sacrifice, or His claim on their lives. And many people who do know His name don't love Him and take His name in vain, intentionally and unintentionally," Irena explains.

"I'm shocked. I've misunderstood so much for so long. But now that you mention it, it seems right that just because someone makes a casual confession and statement about making the Lord their personal Savior doesn't mean they're saved. I know plenty of people who said they were Christians, but they lived their lives in sin and contempt of God. If they were brought before a court accused of being a Christian, most of them would be found *not guilty*. They lied, cheated, stole, coveted, gossiped, and sinned just as everyone else around them. And there are Muslims and Hindus, Buddhists and Pagans that act out of love and goodness. So, these are spiritual descendants of Abraham, obeying God's law in their hearts; though they don't know God, God knows them. It's like the parable that Jesus talked about the two brothers. One said 'yes' to his father, and the other said 'no,' but their obedience was based not on their words but on their actions, and it was their obedience or lack thereof that defined the quality and character of each son's relationship with his father. This is not to say, however, that those that worship false gods belong to God, rather that God leads His children out of false religions, including some Christians by name only, and into His glorious truth and presence," Karen posits.

"The Lord's atonement is applied to whomever He applies it. Half a billion aborted babies are saved by the application of atonement, even though the infants never knew the Lord's name or made any decision in response to the Lord's offer of salvation. In the same way, whomever the Lord elects and in whatever manner the Lord elects, it is the business of God, not man," replies Irena. "Depart in peace, my loved ones."

The companions resume their journey and come to a village named Morning Star, where, after being greeted, it's suggested that they repast at Ollie's Coffeehouse. The coffeehouse is located at the western edge of the village, near a cliff that yields a magnificent view of Gallant Forest below. Morning Star has narrow winding roads of delicately woven pavers with much flowering and fruiting flora above and at street level. Storefront sections are interspersed between residential sections and numerous parks. The coffeehouse has an engraved wooden shingle with what appears to be a real (giant-sized) cup of coffee that passers-by can smell as steam aromatically rises from the brim of the cup.

The company enters and finds an inside table with a view of the majestic wood below. Ollie notices the group, walks over to their table, and asks, "Is there one in the troupe named Karen?" Karen responds, and he indicates that he has an item for Karen and that he'll be right back with it.

In the meantime, they're served coffee, tea, and lovely dainties. Soft live music is playing in the background—Karen wonders if the musicians take requests. "I'm going to ask them if they take requests," Karen says to Nora excitedly. Karen gets up from the table and approaches the musicians. When they reach a stopping point, she says, "Your music is lovely. Thank you for playing. Do you take requests?"

"We've never been asked that, but I suppose we do. What would you like to hear, sister?" the guitarist responds.

"Well, since this is a coffeehouse, I'd love to hear the *Java Jive*. Do you know it?"

"No, I mean yes. Yes, we do know it, somehow. It's a great tune! We'd love to play this. Thanks for requesting, sister," the band concurs.

Not three measures into the tune, and the house is rocking. Already standing and shuffling to the beat, Karen breaks into full dance mode. Several others join in the dance. Karen grabs Ollie as he walks by, and they dance the song to its conclusion. Ollie remarks, "This is my favorite song from now on."

Karen and Ollie return to the table, and he hands over an irregularly shaped object wrapped in some form of linen paper to Karen. Karen unwraps the item (with the coaxing of the others) and reveals it to be a scroll. The companions puzzle over it for a bit, then a stranger, another coffeehouse patron, walks over and says, "God has a message for the companions: 'This gift is a quest. The quest is optional, the risks are great, and the eternal lives of souls lay in the balance.'"

It's not the first quest given in Paradise, nor will it be the last, but it's specific to Karen's company. If they choose to embark on the quest, they must complete it to whatever conclusion and do so together. The stranger also tells them that if they decide to undertake the quest, "one other person will be added to the company for good or ill."

The company asks, "What does all this mean?" And "Why does it sound so ominous?" "What is meant by the 'Fate of souls hangs in the balance?'" And "Is this new companion going to help or hurt us?"

The stranger says, "I have no further information. I'm sorry, but I can advise you no further." Then, as they continue asking questions of one another, he politely departs. "My mission is accomplished," he says, just as AJ appears.

Claude's enthusiasm is childlike and contagious, but reason starts to set in, and the ladies begin to cool to the idea of a quest. Each person, in turn, looks over to AJ. AJ responds, "I have no idea what's going on. I haven't been told anything. Apparently, I'm as much a part of the quest as you all are and equally in the dark."

The companions discuss the quest—the risks without knowing the payoff cause Karen and Nora to hesitate; however, Claude is enthusiastically supportive. AJ abstains; he'll support Karen's and the company's decision without reservation. The company departs the coffeehouse, uncertain whether to accept the quest.

Just outside the village, Karen has another episode of grief, and then Nora asks the company whether the purpose of the quest is to redress Karen's plight. They respond that they don't know, but they do know that God is good and He "doesn't give a stone when his child asks for bread," and Karen can't go on this way. They must do something. The companions decide to undertake the quest but don't know how to take the first step.

As they reenter the Gallant Forest, they only get past the next village on the road to Servan'ya when they encounter a man intercepting them from a side road. He introduces himself as Blaise and says he was told by an angel that God had a mission for him, and he was to come to this spot and join a *party of seekers*.

"I was given no further information except that Karen is the seeker and her companions are co-seekers. Are you the seekers? Is one of you Karen?" asks the man. The group responds and welcomes him into the company. Blaise begins to ask lots of questions. "What are you seeking? Why? Where? What information do you have? What's your plan?"

Claude gets annoyed and counters, "You've only just got here. You know nothing about the quest and act like God's gift to the fellowship."

"I'm sorry. I meant no offense, but let me approach this from another perspective. Karen and each of us have been given a task by

God, a quest you called it. You have been given some instructions and directions you don't understand. And you have, as of yet, no plan. Do I distort the facts, or does that adequately sum up the current situation?" asks Blaise.

"We don't need a plan. God will guide us by our feelings and tell us what we need to know when we need to know it," responds Claude.

"Gentlemen," AJ butts in, "clearly, it's become apparent what God is doing here. He has provided the company with an artist and a scientist. Therefore, it seems that our quest will be broad in scope, challenging, and require both subjective and objective reasoning if we are to triumph."

"Yes!" responds the ladies.

"At first, I thought you were okay, AJ," says Claude.

"Why do you say that?" asks AJ.

"Because objective truth is about as creative and interesting as a rock. I can't believe God would limit Himself by operating in an objective domain. God is an artist, like me, well, not like me, but you know what I mean."

"Yes," the group concurs.

"God is an artist," Blaise concurs but reserves his value-add.

Karen says, "No doubt God is the artist, but even artists plan a painting or sculpture. I think, Claude, you're correct in that God will provide. But I think his provision is, as AJ said—a balance between art and science; I think we need a plan. I think God has provided both Claude and Blaise."

"I have no objection to a plan. I just don't feel it should come from a machine," continues Claude.

"Before we can architect the plan, we first need to explore what information we currently have and gain a shared understanding of what it means; we call that the *As Is Analysis* phase. Next, we'll need to define the gaps in our knowledge. We call that a *Gap Analysis* phase. Then, we will need to define potential approaches to redress the gaps. We call this the *Solutioning* phase, and we prioritize the solutions, size the costs of deploying the solutions, and decide which solutions yield the best chance of success at the lowest costs and risks. Once we complete these analyses, we'll be able to formulate a plan," Blaise remarks.

"This is going to be a nightmare in Paradise," adds Claude. "By the time we've conducted all this turning of gears, the Second Coming will have come and gone."

"Can't we just skip some steps and get right to the plan?" asks Nora.

"No, we must proceed via the scientific method," responds Blaise. Blaise takes the team through what's known, and they identify the gaps, then they prioritize and make a plan. In the end, Karen says, "God is good and always right. I don't think like that. I never would have been able to march through all these complex mechanics and figure out a plan."

"Well, I must admit, the scientific method may have some minimal usefulness in a narrow spectrum of circumstances," remarks Claude.

Nora asks Blaise who he is if she would "recognize his name and contribution to science?"

Blaise responds, "I am not worthy of being mentioned or remembered in the halls of science."

AJ adds that his name is Blaise Pascal, and God greatly loves him. He was quite the mathematical prodigy and dabbled in physics, and he eventually helped formalize the scientific method for all humanity. "So, you see, God has blessed the company with a balance between one of the greatest scientific minds and one of the most extraordinary artistic hearts. No matter what challenges this quest holds, God has given us at least a fighting chance—assuming the artist

E. Vince

and the scientist don't destroy each other before the quest can be completed!" remarks AJ.

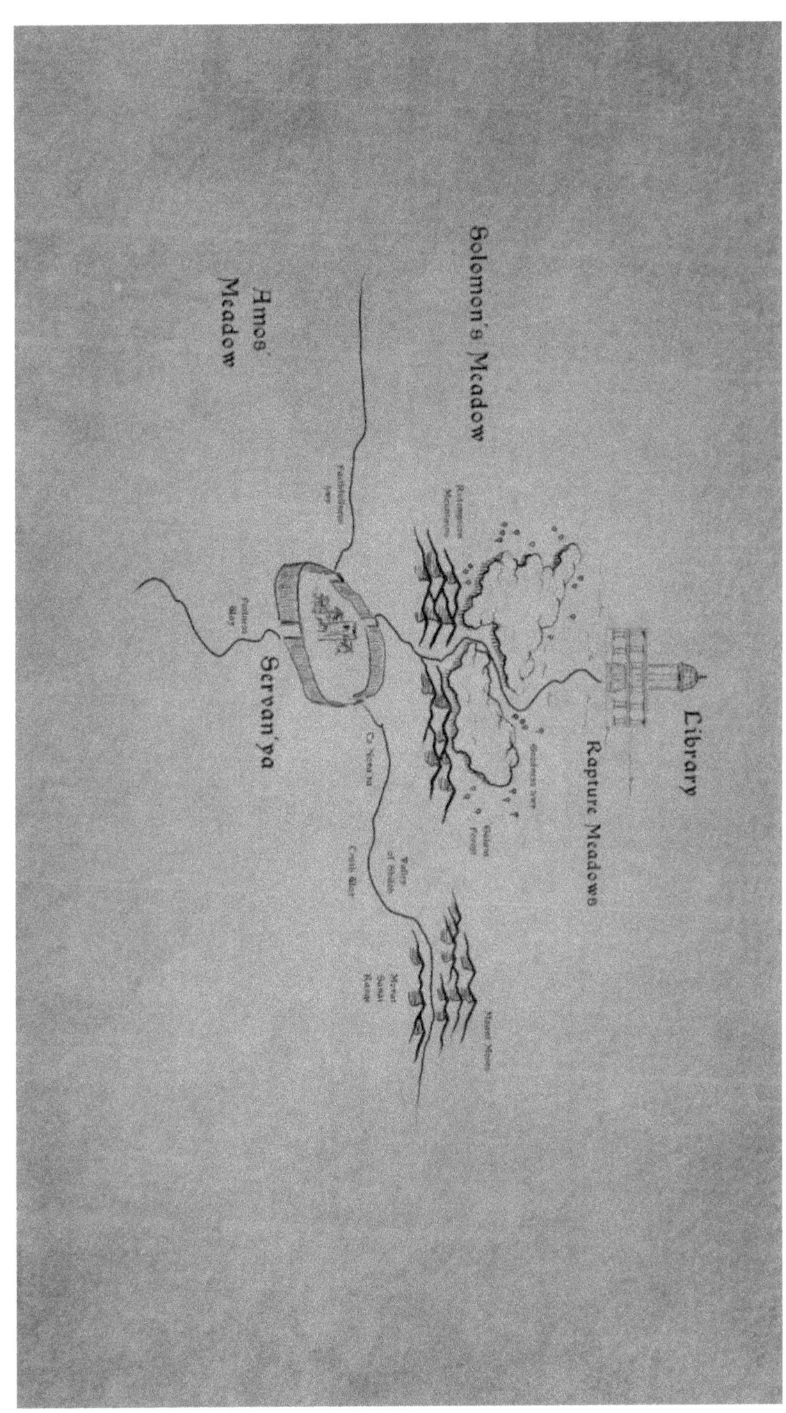

Figure 4 Road to Servan'ya

203